SAXON MATH

Course 2

Power Up
Workbook

Stephen Hake

Image Credits: (Paper background pieces) ©Kittichai/Shutterstock and ©Thinglass/Shutterstock; (hermit crab) inhauscreative/E+/Getty Images; (brown shells) drasa/Shutterstock; (orange shells) Alexander Raths/Shutterstock; (starfish) Peteri/Shutterstock.

Copyright © by Houghton Mifflin Harcourt Publishing Company

All rights reserved. No part of this work may be reproduced or transmitted in any form or by any means, electronic or mechanical, including photocopying or recording, or by any information storage or retrieval system, without the prior written permission of the copyright owner unless such copying is expressly permitted by federal copyright law. Requests for permission to make copies of any part of the work should be submitted through our Permissions website at https://customercare.hmhco.com/contactus/Permissions.html or mailed to Houghton Mifflin Harcourt Publishing Company, Attn: Intellectual Property Licensing, 9400 Southpark Center Loop, Orlando, Florida 32819-8647.

Printed in the U.S.A.

ISBN   978-1-328-49748-2

1 2 3 4 5 6 7 8 9 10   0982   26 25 24 23 22 21 20 19 18

4500708967   A B C D E F G

If you have received these materials as examination copies free of charge, Houghton Mifflin Harcourt Publishing Company retains title to the materials and they may not be resold. Resale of examination copies is strictly prohibited.

Possession of this publication in print format does not entitle users to convert this publication, or any portion of it, into electronic format.

Dear Student,

We enjoy watching the adventures of "Super Heroes" because they have powers that they use for good. Power is the ability to get things done. We acquire power through concentrated effort and practice. We build powerful bodies with vigorous exercise and healthy living. We develop powerful minds by learning and using skills that help us understand the world around us and solve problems that come our way.

We can build our mathematical power in several ways. We can use our memory to store and instantly recall frequently used information. We can improve our ability to solve many kinds of problems mentally without using pencil and paper or a calculator. We can also expand the range of strategies we use to approach and solve new problems.

The Power Up section of each lesson in *Saxon Math Course 2* is designed to build your mathematical power. Each Power Up has three parts: Facts Practice, Mental Math, and Problem Solving. The three parts are printed on every Power Up page where you will record your answers. This workbook contains a Power Up page for every lesson.

Facts Practice is like a race—write the answers as fast as you can without making mistakes. If the information in the Facts Practice is new to you, take time to study the information so that you can recall the facts quickly and can complete the exercise faster next time.

Mental Math is the ability to work with numbers in your head. This skill greatly improves with practice. Each lesson includes several mental math problems. Your teacher will read these to you or ask you to read them in your book. Do your best to find the answer to each problem without using pencil and paper, except to record your answers. Strong mental math ability will help you throughout your life.

Problem Solving is like a puzzle. You need to figure out how to solve each puzzle. There are many different strategies you can use to solve problems. There are also some questions you can ask yourself to better understand a problem and come up with a plan to solve it. Your teacher will guide you through the problem each day. Becoming a good problem solver is a superior skill that is highly rewarded.

The Power Ups will help you excel at math and acquire math power that will serve you well for the rest of your life.

Stephen Hake
Temple City, California

Power Up Workbook

Name _____

Facts Practice

Power Up Facts	# Possible	Time and Score 												
A 40 Multiplication Facts	40													
B 20 Equations	20													
C 20 Improper Fractions and Mixed Numbers	20													
D 20 Fractions to Reduce	20													
E Circles	12													
F Lines, Angles, Polygons	12													
G + − × ÷ Fractions	16													
H Measurement Facts	30													
I Proportions	15													
J + − × ÷ Decimals	16													
K Powers and Roots	20													
L Fraction-Decimal-Percent Equivalents	24													
M Metric Conversions	22													
N + − × ÷ Mixed Numbers	16													
O Classifying Quadrilaterals and Triangles	8													
P + − × ÷ Integers	16													
Q Percent-Decimal-Fraction Equivalents	24													
R Area	8													
S Scientific Notation	12													
T Order of Operations	8													
U Two-Step Equations	12													
V + − × ÷ Algebraic Terms	16													
W Multiplying and Dividing in Scientific Notation	12													

 Harcourt Achieve Inc. and Stephen Hake. All rights reserved

Facts   Multiply.

9 × 8	8 × 2	10 × 10	6 × 3	4 × 2	5 × 5	9 × 9	6 × 4	9 × 6	7 × 3
9 × 3	6 × 5	0 × 0	7 × 6	8 × 8	7 × 4	5 × 3	9 × 7	2 × 2	8 × 6
7 × 7	6 × 2	4 × 3	8 × 5	4 × 4	3 × 2	n × 0	8 × 4	6 × 6	9 × 2
8 × 3	5 × 4	n × 1	7 × 2	9 × 5	8 × 7	3 × 3	9 × 4	5 × 2	7 × 5

Mental Math

a.	b.	c.	d.
e.	**f.**	**g.**	**h.**

Problem Solving

Understand
What information am I given?
What am I asked to find or do?

- -

Plan
How can I use the information I am given?
Which strategy should I try?

- -

Solve
Did I follow the plan?
Did I show my work?
Did I write the answer?

- -

Check
Did I use the correct information?
Did I do what was asked?
Is my answer reasonable?

© Houghton Mifflin Harcourt Publishing Company and Stephen Hake

Facts Multiply.

9 ×8	8 ×2	10 ×10	6 ×3	4 ×2	5 ×5	9 ×9	6 ×4	9 ×6	7 ×3
9 ×3	6 ×5	0 ×0	7 ×6	8 ×8	7 ×4	5 ×3	9 ×7	2 ×2	8 ×6
7 ×7	6 ×2	4 ×3	8 ×5	4 ×4	3 ×2	n ×0	8 ×4	6 ×6	9 ×2
8 ×3	5 ×4	n ×1	7 ×2	9 ×5	8 ×7	3 ×3	9 ×4	5 ×2	7 ×5

Mental Math

a.	b.	c.	d.
e.	f.	g.	h.

Problem Solving

Understand
What information am I given?
What am I asked to find or do?

- -

Plan
How can I use the information I am given?
Which strategy should I try?

- -

Solve
Did I follow the plan?
Did I show my work?
Did I write the answer?

- -

Check
Did I use the correct information?
Did I do what was asked?
Is my answer reasonable?

© Houghton Mifflin Harcourt Publishing Company and Stephen Hake

Name _____ Time _____

Facts   Multiply.

9 × 8	8 × 2	10 × 10	6 × 3	4 × 2	5 × 5	9 × 9	6 × 4	9 × 6	7 × 3
9 × 3	6 × 5	0 × 0	7 × 6	8 × 8	7 × 4	5 × 3	9 × 7	2 × 2	8 × 6
7 × 7	6 × 2	4 × 3	8 × 5	4 × 4	3 × 2	n × 0	8 × 4	6 × 6	9 × 2
8 × 3	5 × 4	n × 1	7 × 2	9 × 5	8 × 7	3 × 3	9 × 4	5 × 2	7 × 5

Mental Math

a.	b.	c.	d.
e.	**f.**	**g.**	**h.**

Problem Solving

Understand

What information am I given?

What am I asked to find or do?

- -

Plan

How can I use the information I am given?

Which strategy should I try?

- -

Solve

Did I follow the plan?

Did I show my work?

Did I write the answer?

- -

Check

Did I use the correct information?

Did I do what was asked?

Is my answer reasonable?

© Houghton Mifflin Harcourt Publishing Company and Stephen Hake

Facts   Multiply.

9 × 8	8 × 2	10 × 10	6 × 3	4 × 2	5 × 5	9 × 9	6 × 4	9 × 6	7 × 3
9 × 3	6 × 5	0 × 0	7 × 6	8 × 8	7 × 4	5 × 3	9 × 7	2 × 2	8 × 6
7 × 7	6 × 2	4 × 3	8 × 5	4 × 4	3 × 2	n × 0	8 × 4	6 × 6	9 × 2
8 × 3	5 × 4	n × 1	7 × 2	9 × 5	8 × 7	3 × 3	9 × 4	5 × 2	7 × 5

Mental Math

a.	b.	c.	d.
e.	f.	g.	h.

Problem Solving

Understand

What information am I given?

What am I asked to find or do?

- -

Plan

How can I use the information I am given?

Which strategy should I try?

- -

Solve

Did I follow the plan?

Did I show my work?

Did I write the answer?

- -

Check

Did I use the correct information?

Did I do what was asked?

Is my answer reasonable?

© Houghton Mifflin Harcourt Publishing Company and Stephen Hake

Facts   Multiply.

9 × 8	8 × 2	10 × 10	6 × 3	4 × 2	5 × 5	9 × 9	6 × 4	9 × 6	7 × 3
9 × 3	6 × 5	0 × 0	7 × 6	8 × 8	7 × 4	5 × 3	9 × 7	2 × 2	8 × 6
7 × 7	6 × 2	4 × 3	8 × 5	4 × 4	3 × 2	n × 0	8 × 4	6 × 6	9 × 2
8 × 3	5 × 4	n × 1	7 × 2	9 × 5	8 × 7	3 × 3	9 × 4	5 × 2	7 × 5

Mental Math

a.	**b.**	**c.**	**d.**
e.	**f.**	**g.**	**h.**

Problem Solving

Understand

What information am I given?

What am I asked to find or do?

- -

Plan

How can I use the information I am given?

Which strategy should I try?

- -

Solve

Did I follow the plan?

Did I show my work?

Did I write the answer?

- -

Check

Did I use the correct information?

Did I do what was asked?

Is my answer reasonable?

© Houghton Mifflin Harcourt Publishing Company and Stephen Hake

Facts   Solve each equation.

$a + 12 = 20$ $a =$	$b - 8 = 10$ $b =$	$5c = 40$ $c =$	$\dfrac{d}{4} = 12$ $d =$	$11 + e = 24$ $e =$
$25 - f = 10$ $f =$	$10g = 60$ $g =$	$\dfrac{24}{h} = 6$ $h =$	$15 = j + 8$ $j =$	$20 = k - 5$ $k =$
$30 = 6m$ $m =$	$9 = \dfrac{n}{3}$ $n =$	$18 = 6 + p$ $p =$	$5 = 15 - q$ $q =$	$36 = 4r$ $r =$
$2 = \dfrac{16}{s}$ $s =$	$t + 8 = 12$ $t =$	$u - 15 = 30$ $u =$	$8v = 48$ $v =$	$\dfrac{w}{3} = 6$ $w =$

Mental Math

a.	**b.**	**c.**	**d.**
e.	**f.**	**g.**	**h.**

Problem Solving

Understand

What information am I given?
What am I asked to find or do?

- -

Plan

How can I use the information I am given?
Which strategy should I try?

- -

Solve

Did I follow the plan?
Did I show my work?
Did I write the answer?

- -

Check

Did I use the correct information?
Did I do what was asked?
Is my answer reasonable?

© Houghton Mifflin Harcourt Publishing Company and Stephen Hake

Facts   Solve each equation.

$a + 12 = 20$ $a =$	$b - 8 = 10$ $b =$	$5c = 40$ $c =$	$\dfrac{d}{4} = 12$ $d =$	$11 + e = 24$ $e =$
$25 - f = 10$ $f =$	$10g = 60$ $g =$	$\dfrac{24}{h} = 6$ $h =$	$15 = j + 8$ $j =$	$20 = k - 5$ $k =$
$30 = 6m$ $m =$	$9 = \dfrac{n}{3}$ $n =$	$18 = 6 + p$ $p =$	$5 = 15 - q$ $q =$	$36 = 4r$ $r =$
$2 = \dfrac{16}{s}$ $s =$	$t + 8 = 12$ $t =$	$u - 15 = 30$ $u =$	$8v = 48$ $v =$	$\dfrac{w}{3} = 6$ $w =$

Mental Math

a.	**b.**	**c.**	**d.**
e.	**f.**	**g.**	**h.**

Problem Solving

Understand
What information am I given?
What am I asked to find or do?

Plan
How can I use the information I am given?
Which strategy should I try?

Solve
Did I follow the plan?
Did I show my work?
Did I write the answer?

Check
Did I use the correct information?
Did I do what was asked?
Is my answer reasonable?

© Houghton Mifflin Harcourt Publishing Company and Stephen Hake

Name _____ Time _____

Facts Multiply.

9 $\times 8$	8 $\times 2$	10 $\times 10$	6 $\times 3$	4 $\times 2$	5 $\times 5$	9 $\times 9$	6 $\times 4$	9 $\times 6$	7 $\times 3$
9 $\times 3$	6 $\times 5$	0 $\times 0$	7 $\times 6$	8 $\times 8$	7 $\times 4$	5 $\times 3$	9 $\times 7$	2 $\times 2$	8 $\times 6$
7 $\times 7$	6 $\times 2$	4 $\times 3$	8 $\times 5$	4 $\times 4$	3 $\times 2$	n $\times 0$	8 $\times 4$	6 $\times 6$	9 $\times 2$
8 $\times 3$	5 $\times 4$	n $\times 1$	7 $\times 2$	9 $\times 5$	8 $\times 7$	3 $\times 3$	9 $\times 4$	5 $\times 2$	7 $\times 5$

Mental Math

a.	**b.**	**c.**	**d.**
e.	**f.**	**g.**	**h.**

Problem Solving

Understand
What information am I given?
What am I asked to find or do?

- -

Plan
How can I use the information I am given?
Which strategy should I try?

- -

Solve
Did I follow the plan?
Did I show my work?
Did I write the answer?

- -

Check
Did I use the correct information?
Did I do what was asked?
Is my answer reasonable?

© Houghton Mifflin Harcourt Publishing Company and Stephen Hake

Facts — Multiply.

9 ×8	8 ×2	10 ×10	6 ×3	4 ×2	5 ×5	9 ×9	6 ×4	9 ×6	7 ×3
9 ×3	6 ×5	0 ×0	7 ×6	8 ×8	7 ×4	5 ×3	9 ×7	2 ×2	8 ×6
7 ×7	6 ×2	4 ×3	8 ×5	4 ×4	3 ×2	n ×0	8 ×4	6 ×6	9 ×2
8 ×3	5 ×4	n ×1	7 ×2	9 ×5	8 ×7	3 ×3	9 ×4	5 ×2	7 ×5

Mental Math

a.	b.	c.	d.
e.	f.	g.	h.

Problem Solving

Understand

What information am I given?
What am I asked to find or do?

Plan

How can I use the information I am given?
Which strategy should I try?

Solve

Did I follow the plan?
Did I show my work?
Did I write the answer?

Check

Did I use the correct information?
Did I do what was asked?
Is my answer reasonable?

© Houghton Mifflin Harcourt Publishing Company and Stephen Hake

Facts   Multiply.

9 ×8	8 ×2	10 ×10	6 ×3	4 ×2	5 ×5	9 ×9	6 ×4	9 ×6	7 ×3
9 ×3	6 ×5	0 ×0	7 ×6	8 ×8	7 ×4	5 ×3	9 ×7	2 ×2	8 ×6
7 ×7	6 ×2	4 ×3	8 ×5	4 ×4	3 ×2	n ×0	8 ×4	6 ×6	9 ×2
8 ×3	5 ×4	n ×1	7 ×2	9 ×5	8 ×7	3 ×3	9 ×4	5 ×2	7 ×5

Mental Math

a.	b.	c.	d.
e.	f.	g.	h.

Problem Solving

Understand
What information am I given?
What am I asked to find or do?

Plan
How can I use the information I am given?
Which strategy should I try?

Solve
Did I follow the plan?
Did I show my work?
Did I write the answer?

Check
Did I use the correct information?
Did I do what was asked?
Is my answer reasonable?

© Houghton Mifflin Harcourt Publishing Company and Stephen Hake

Facts — Write each improper fraction as a whole number or mixed number.

$\frac{5}{2} =$	$\frac{7}{4} =$	$\frac{12}{5} =$	$\frac{10}{3} =$	$\frac{15}{2} =$
$\frac{15}{5} =$	$\frac{11}{8} =$	$2\frac{3}{2} =$	$4\frac{5}{4} =$	$3\frac{7}{4} =$

Write each mixed number as an improper fraction.

$1\frac{1}{2} =$	$2\frac{2}{3} =$	$3\frac{3}{4} =$	$2\frac{1}{2} =$	$6\frac{2}{3} =$
$2\frac{3}{4} =$	$3\frac{1}{3} =$	$4\frac{1}{2} =$	$1\frac{7}{8} =$	$12\frac{1}{2} =$

Mental Math

a.	b.	c.	d.
e.	f.	g.	h.

Problem Solving

Understand
What information am I given?
What am I asked to find or do?

- -

Plan
How can I use the information I am given?
Which strategy should I try?

- -

Solve
Did I follow the plan?
Did I show my work?
Did I write the answer?

- -

Check
Did I use the correct information?
Did I do what was asked?
Is my answer reasonable?

© Houghton Mifflin Harcourt Publishing Company and Stephen Hake

Facts Write each improper fraction as a whole number or mixed number.

$\frac{5}{2}=$	$\frac{7}{4}=$	$\frac{12}{5}=$	$\frac{10}{3}=$	$\frac{15}{2}=$
$\frac{15}{5}=$	$\frac{11}{8}=$	$2\frac{3}{2}=$	$4\frac{5}{4}=$	$3\frac{7}{4}=$

Write each mixed number as an improper fraction.

$1\frac{1}{2}=$	$2\frac{2}{3}=$	$3\frac{3}{4}=$	$2\frac{1}{2}=$	$6\frac{2}{3}=$
$2\frac{3}{4}=$	$3\frac{1}{3}=$	$4\frac{1}{2}=$	$1\frac{7}{8}=$	$12\frac{1}{2}=$

Mental Math

a.	b.	c.	d.
e.	f.	g.	h.

Problem Solving

Understand
What information am I given?
What am I asked to find or do?

Plan
How can I use the information I am given?
Which strategy should I try?

Solve
Did I follow the plan?
Did I show my work?
Did I write the answer?

Check
Did I use the correct information?
Did I do what was asked?
Is my answer reasonable?

© Houghton Mifflin Harcourt Publishing Company and Stephen Hake

Saxon Math Course 2

Name _____ Time _____

Facts	Write each improper fraction as a whole number or mixed number.			
$\frac{5}{2} =$	$\frac{7}{4} =$	$\frac{12}{5} =$	$\frac{10}{3} =$	$\frac{15}{2} =$
$\frac{15}{5} =$	$\frac{11}{8} =$	$2\frac{3}{2} =$	$4\frac{5}{4} =$	$3\frac{7}{4} =$

Write each mixed number as an improper fraction.

$1\frac{1}{2} =$	$2\frac{2}{3} =$	$3\frac{3}{4} =$	$2\frac{1}{2} =$	$6\frac{2}{3} =$
$2\frac{3}{4} =$	$3\frac{1}{3} =$	$4\frac{1}{2} =$	$1\frac{7}{8} =$	$12\frac{1}{2} =$

Mental Math			
a.	b.	c.	d.
e.	f.	g.	h.

Problem Solving

Understand
What information am I given?
What am I asked to find or do?

- -

Plan
How can I use the information I am given?
Which strategy should I try?

- -

Solve
Did I follow the plan?
Did I show my work?
Did I write the answer?

- -

Check
Did I use the correct information?
Did I do what was asked?
Is my answer reasonable?

© Houghton Mifflin Harcourt Publishing Company and Stephen Hake

Saxon Math Course 2

Name _____ Time _____

Facts   Multiply.

9 × 8	8 × 2	10 × 10	6 × 3	4 × 2	5 × 5	9 × 9	6 × 4	9 × 6	7 × 3
9 × 3	6 × 5	0 × 0	7 × 6	8 × 8	7 × 4	5 × 3	9 × 7	2 × 2	8 × 6
7 × 7	6 × 2	4 × 3	8 × 5	4 × 4	3 × 2	n × 0	8 × 4	6 × 6	9 × 2
8 × 3	5 × 4	n × 1	7 × 2	9 × 5	8 × 7	3 × 3	9 × 4	5 × 2	7 × 5

Mental Math

a.	**b.**	**c.**	**d.**
e.	**f.**	**g.**	**h.**

Problem Solving

Understand

What information am I given?

What am I asked to find or do?

- -

Plan

How can I use the information I am given?

Which strategy should I try?

- -

Solve

Did I follow the plan?

Did I show my work?

Did I write the answer?

- -

Check

Did I use the correct information?

Did I do what was asked?

Is my answer reasonable?

© Houghton Mifflin Harcourt Publishing Company and Stephen Hake

Facts	Write each improper fraction as a whole number or mixed number.			
$\frac{5}{2} =$	$\frac{7}{4} =$	$\frac{12}{5} =$	$\frac{10}{3} =$	$\frac{15}{2} =$
$\frac{15}{5} =$	$\frac{11}{8} =$	$2\frac{3}{2} =$	$4\frac{5}{4} =$	$3\frac{7}{4} =$

Write each mixed number as an improper fraction.

$1\frac{1}{2} =$	$2\frac{2}{3} =$	$3\frac{3}{4} =$	$2\frac{1}{2} =$	$6\frac{2}{3} =$
$2\frac{3}{4} =$	$3\frac{1}{3} =$	$4\frac{1}{2} =$	$1\frac{7}{8} =$	$12\frac{1}{2} =$

Mental Math

a.	b.	c.	d.
e.	f.	g.	h.

Problem Solving

Understand

What information am I given?

What am I asked to find or do?

- -

Plan

How can I use the information I am given?

Which strategy should I try?

- -

Solve

Did I follow the plan?

Did I show my work?

Did I write the answer?

- -

Check

Did I use the correct information?

Did I do what was asked?

Is my answer reasonable?

© Houghton Mifflin Harcourt Publishing Company and Stephen Hake

Facts	Reduce each fraction to lowest terms.			
$\frac{50}{100} =$	$\frac{4}{16} =$	$\frac{6}{8} =$	$\frac{8}{12} =$	$\frac{10}{100} =$
$\frac{8}{16} =$	$\frac{20}{100} =$	$\frac{3}{12} =$	$\frac{60}{100} =$	$\frac{9}{12} =$
$\frac{6}{9} =$	$\frac{90}{100} =$	$\frac{5}{10} =$	$\frac{12}{16} =$	$\frac{25}{100} =$
$\frac{4}{10} =$	$\frac{4}{6} =$	$\frac{75}{100} =$	$\frac{4}{12} =$	$\frac{6}{10} =$

Mental Math			
a.	**b.**	**c.**	**d.**
e.	**f.**	**g.**	**h.**

Problem Solving

Understand
What information am I given?
What am I asked to find or do?

- -

Plan
How can I use the information I am given?
Which strategy should I try?

- -

Solve
Did I follow the plan?
Did I show my work?
Did I write the answer?

- -

Check
Did I use the correct information?
Did I do what was asked?
Is my answer reasonable?

© Houghton Mifflin Harcourt Publishing Company and Stephen Hake

Facts	Reduce each fraction to lowest terms.			
$\frac{50}{100} =$	$\frac{4}{16} =$	$\frac{6}{8} =$	$\frac{8}{12} =$	$\frac{10}{100} =$
$\frac{8}{16} =$	$\frac{20}{100} =$	$\frac{3}{12} =$	$\frac{60}{100} =$	$\frac{9}{12} =$
$\frac{6}{9} =$	$\frac{90}{100} =$	$\frac{5}{10} =$	$\frac{12}{16} =$	$\frac{25}{100} =$
$\frac{4}{10} =$	$\frac{4}{6} =$	$\frac{75}{100} =$	$\frac{4}{12} =$	$\frac{6}{10} =$

Mental Math			
a.	**b.**	**c.**	**d.**
e.	**f.**	**g.**	**h.**

Problem Solving

Understand
What information am I given?
What am I asked to find or do?

Plan
How can I use the information I am given?
Which strategy should I try?

Solve
Did I follow the plan?
Did I show my work?
Did I write the answer?

Check
Did I use the correct information?
Did I do what was asked?
Is my answer reasonable?

© Houghton Mifflin Harcourt Publishing Company and Stephen Hake

Facts	Reduce each fraction to lowest terms.			
$\frac{50}{100} =$	$\frac{4}{16} =$	$\frac{6}{8} =$	$\frac{8}{12} =$	$\frac{10}{100} =$
$\frac{8}{16} =$	$\frac{20}{100} =$	$\frac{3}{12} =$	$\frac{60}{100} =$	$\frac{9}{12} =$
$\frac{6}{9} =$	$\frac{90}{100} =$	$\frac{5}{10} =$	$\frac{12}{16} =$	$\frac{25}{100} =$
$\frac{4}{10} =$	$\frac{4}{6} =$	$\frac{75}{100} =$	$\frac{4}{12} =$	$\frac{6}{10} =$

Mental Math			
a.	**b.**	**c.**	**d.**
e.	**f.**	**g.**	**h.**

Problem Solving

Understand

What information am I given?

What am I asked to find or do?

- -

Plan

How can I use the information I am given?

Which strategy should I try?

- -

Solve

Did I follow the plan?

Did I show my work?

Did I write the answer?

- -

Check

Did I use the correct information?

Did I do what was asked?

Is my answer reasonable?

© Houghton Mifflin Harcourt Publishing Company and Stephen Hake

Name _____ Time _____

| **Facts** | Write each improper fraction as a whole number or mixed number. ||||

$\frac{5}{2} =$	$\frac{7}{4} =$	$\frac{12}{5} =$	$\frac{10}{3} =$	$\frac{15}{2} =$
$\frac{15}{5} =$	$\frac{11}{8} =$	$2\frac{3}{2} =$	$4\frac{5}{4} =$	$3\frac{7}{4} =$

Write each mixed number as an improper fraction.

$1\frac{1}{2} =$	$2\frac{2}{3} =$	$3\frac{3}{4} =$	$2\frac{1}{2} =$	$6\frac{2}{3} =$
$2\frac{3}{4} =$	$3\frac{1}{3} =$	$4\frac{1}{2} =$	$1\frac{7}{8} =$	$12\frac{1}{2} =$

Mental Math

a.	b.	c.	d.
e.	f.	g.	h.

Problem Solving

Understand
What information am I given?
What am I asked to find or do?

- -

Plan
How can I use the information I am given?
Which strategy should I try?

- -

Solve
Did I follow the plan?
Did I show my work?
Did I write the answer?

- -

Check
Did I use the correct information?
Did I do what was asked?
Is my answer reasonable?

© Houghton Mifflin Harcourt Publishing Company and Stephen Hake

Facts	Reduce each fraction to lowest terms.

$\frac{50}{100} =$	$\frac{4}{16} =$	$\frac{6}{8} =$	$\frac{8}{12} =$	$\frac{10}{100} =$
$\frac{8}{16} =$	$\frac{20}{100} =$	$\frac{3}{12} =$	$\frac{60}{100} =$	$\frac{9}{12} =$
$\frac{6}{9} =$	$\frac{90}{100} =$	$\frac{5}{10} =$	$\frac{12}{16} =$	$\frac{25}{100} =$
$\frac{4}{10} =$	$\frac{4}{6} =$	$\frac{75}{100} =$	$\frac{4}{12} =$	$\frac{6}{10} =$

Mental Math

a.	**b.**	**c.**	**d.**
e.	**f.**	**g.**	**h.**

Problem Solving

Understand

What information am I given?

What am I asked to find or do?

- -

Plan

How can I use the information I am given?

Which strategy should I try?

- -

Solve

Did I follow the plan?

Did I show my work?

Did I write the answer?

- -

Check

Did I use the correct information?

Did I do what was asked?

Is my answer reasonable?

© Houghton Mifflin Harcourt Publishing Company and Stephen Hake

Facts   Write the word or words to complete each definition.

The distance around a circle is its _____.	Every point on a circle is the same distance from its _____.	The distance across a circle through its center is its _____.	The distance from a circle to its center is its _____.
Two or more circles with the same center are _____.	A segment between two points on a circle is a _____.	Part of a circumference is an _____.	Part of a circle bounded by an arc and two radii is a _____.
Half a circle is a _____.	An angle whose vertex is the center of a circle is a _____.	An angle whose vertex is on the circle and whose sides include chords is an _____.	A polygon whose vertices are on the circle and whose edges are within the circle is an _____.

Mental Math

a.	b.	c.	d.
e.	f.	g.	h.

Problem Solving

Understand
What information am I given?
What am I asked to find or do?

Plan
How can I use the information I am given?
Which strategy should I try?

Solve
Did I follow the plan?
Did I show my work?
Did I write the answer?

Check
Did I use the correct information?
Did I do what was asked?
Is my answer reasonable?

© Houghton Mifflin Harcourt Publishing Company and Stephen Hake

Name _____ Time _____

Facts   Write the word or words to complete each definition.

The distance around a circle is its _____.	Every point on a circle is the same distance from its _____.	The distance across a circle through its center is its _____.	The distance from a circle to its center is its _____.
Two or more circles with the same center are _____.	A segment between two points on a circle is a _____.	Part of a circumference is an _____.	Part of a circle bounded by an arc and two radii is a _____.
Half a circle is a _____.	An angle whose vertex is the center of a circle is a _____.	An angle whose vertex is on the circle and whose sides include chords is an _____.	A polygon whose vertices are on the circle and whose edges are within the circle is an _____.

Mental Math

a.	**b.**	**c.**	**d.**
e.	**f.**	**g.**	**h.**

Problem Solving

Understand
What information am I given?
What am I asked to find or do?

- -

Plan
How can I use the information I am given?
Which strategy should I try?

- -

Solve
Did I follow the plan?
Did I show my work?
Did I write the answer?

- -

Check
Did I use the correct information?
Did I do what was asked?
Is my answer reasonable?

© Houghton Mifflin Harcourt Publishing Company and Stephen Hake

Saxon Math Course 2

Name _____ Time _____

Facts Write the word or words to complete each definition.

The distance around a circle is its _____.	Every point on a circle is the same distance from its _____.	The distance across a circle through its center is its _____.	The distance from a circle to its center is its _____.
Two or more circles with the same center are _____.	A segment between two points on a circle is a _____.	Part of a circumference is an _____.	Part of a circle bounded by an arc and two radii is a _____.
Half a circle is a _____.	An angle whose vertex is the center of a circle is a _____.	An angle whose vertex is on the circle and whose sides include chords is an _____.	A polygon whose vertices are on the circle and whose edges are within the circle is an _____.

Mental Math

a.	b.	c.	d.
e.	f.	g.	h.

Problem Solving

Understand
What information am I given?
What am I asked to find or do?

Plan
How can I use the information I am given?
Which strategy should I try?

Solve
Did I follow the plan?
Did I show my work?
Did I write the answer?

Check
Did I use the correct information?
Did I do what was asked?
Is my answer reasonable?

Saxon Math Course 2

23

Facts	Reduce each fraction to lowest terms.			
$\frac{50}{100} =$	$\frac{4}{16} =$	$\frac{6}{8} =$	$\frac{8}{12} =$	$\frac{10}{100} =$
$\frac{8}{16} =$	$\frac{20}{100} =$	$\frac{3}{12} =$	$\frac{60}{100} =$	$\frac{9}{12} =$
$\frac{6}{9} =$	$\frac{90}{100} =$	$\frac{5}{10} =$	$\frac{12}{16} =$	$\frac{25}{100} =$
$\frac{4}{10} =$	$\frac{4}{6} =$	$\frac{75}{100} =$	$\frac{4}{12} =$	$\frac{6}{10} =$

Mental Math			
a.	**b.**	**c.**	**d.**
e.	**f.**	**g.**	**h.**

Problem Solving

Understand

What information am I given?
What am I asked to find or do?

- -

Plan

How can I use the information I am given?
Which strategy should I try?

- -

Solve

Did I follow the plan?
Did I show my work?
Did I write the answer?

- -

Check

Did I use the correct information?
Did I do what was asked?
Is my answer reasonable?

© Houghton Mifflin Harcourt Publishing Company and Stephen Hake

Facts Name each figure illustrated.

1. _____	2. _____	3. _____	4. _____
5. _____	6. _____	7. _____	8. _____
9. _____	10. _____	11. _____	12. A polygon whose sides are equal in length and whose angles are equal in measure is a _____.

Mental Math

a.	b.	c.	d.
e.	f.	g.	h.

Problem Solving

Understand
What information am I given?
What am I asked to find or do?

Plan
How can I use the information I am given?
Which strategy should I try?

Solve
Did I follow the plan?
Did I show my work?
Did I write the answer?

Check
Did I use the correct information?
Did I do what was asked?
Is my answer reasonable?

© Houghton Mifflin Harcourt Publishing Company and Stephen Hake

Facts   Name each figure illustrated.

1. _____	2. _____	3. _____	4. _____
5. _____	6. _____	7. _____	8. _____
9. _____	10. _____	11. _____	12. A polygon whose sides are equal in length and whose angles are equal in measure is a _____.

Mental Math

a.	b.	c.	d.
e.	f.	g.	h.

Problem Solving

Understand

What information am I given?
What am I asked to find or do?

Plan

How can I use the information I am given?
Which strategy should I try?

Solve

Did I follow the plan?
Did I show my work?
Did I write the answer?

Check

Did I use the correct information?
Did I do what was asked?
Is my answer reasonable?

© Houghton Mifflin Harcourt Publishing Company and Stephen Hake

Saxon Math Course 2

Facts   Write the word or words to complete each definition.

The distance around a circle is its _____.	Every point on a circle is the same distance from its _____.	The distance across a circle through its center is its _____.	The distance from a circle to its center is its _____.
Two or more circles with the same center are _____.	A segment between two points on a circle is a _____.	Part of a circumference is an _____.	Part of a circle bounded by an arc and two radii is a _____.
Half a circle is a _____.	An angle whose vertex is the center of a circle is a _____.	An angle whose vertex is on the circle and whose sides include chords is an _____.	A polygon whose vertices are on the circle and whose edges are within the circle is an _____.

Mental Math

a.	b.	c.	d.
e.	**f.**	**g.**	**h.**

Problem Solving

Understand

What information am I given?
What am I asked to find or do?

- -

Plan

How can I use the information I am given?
Which strategy should I try?

- -

Solve

Did I follow the plan?
Did I show my work?
Did I write the answer?

- -

Check

Did I use the correct information?
Did I do what was asked?
Is my answer reasonable?

© Houghton Mifflin Harcourt Publishing Company and Stephen Hake

Facts   Name each figure illustrated.

1.	2.	3.	4.
___	___	___	___

5.	6.	7.	8.
___	___	___	___

9.	10.	11.	12. A polygon whose sides are equal in length and whose angles are equal in measure is a
___	___	___	_____.

Mental Math

a.	b.	c.	d.
e.	f.	g.	h.

Problem Solving

Understand
What information am I given?
What am I asked to find or do?

Plan
How can I use the information I am given?
Which strategy should I try?

Solve
Did I follow the plan?
Did I show my work?
Did I write the answer?

Check
Did I use the correct information?
Did I do what was asked?
Is my answer reasonable?

© Houghton Mifflin Harcourt Publishing Company and Stephen Hake

Saxon Math Course 2

Name _____ Time _____

Facts   Write the word or words to complete each definition.

The distance around a circle is its _____.	Every point on a circle is the same distance from its _____.	The distance across a circle through its center is its _____.	The distance from a circle to its center is its _____.
Two or more circles with the same center are _____.	A segment between two points on a circle is a _____.	Part of a circumference is an _____.	Part of a circle bounded by an arc and two radii is a _____.
Half a circle is a _____.	An angle whose vertex is the center of a circle is a _____.	An angle whose vertex is on the circle and whose sides include chords is an _____.	A polygon whose vertices are on the circle and whose edges are within the circle is an _____.

Mental Math

| a. | b. | c. | d. |
| e. | f. | g. | h. |

Problem Solving

Understand
What information am I given?
What am I asked to find or do?

Plan
How can I use the information I am given?
Which strategy should I try?

Solve
Did I follow the plan?
Did I show my work?
Did I write the answer?

Check
Did I use the correct information?
Did I do what was asked?
Is my answer reasonable?

© Houghton Mifflin Harcourt Publishing Company and Stephen Hake

Facts   Name each figure illustrated.

1. _____	2. _____	3. _____	4. _____
5. _____	6. _____	7. _____	8. _____
9. _____	10. _____	11. _____	12. A polygon whose sides are equal in length and whose angles are equal in measure is a _____.

Mental Math

a.	b.	c.	d.
e.	f.	g.	h.

Problem Solving

Understand
What information am I given?
What am I asked to find or do?

- -

Plan
How can I use the information I am given?
Which strategy should I try?

- -

Solve
Did I follow the plan?
Did I show my work?
Did I write the answer?

- -

Check
Did I use the correct information?
Did I do what was asked?
Is my answer reasonable?

© Houghton Mifflin Harcourt Publishing Company and Stephen Hake

Saxon Math Course 2

Facts   Simplify.

$\frac{2}{3} + \frac{2}{3} =$	$\frac{2}{3} - \frac{1}{3} =$	$\frac{2}{3} \times \frac{2}{3} =$	$\frac{2}{3} \div \frac{2}{3} =$
$\frac{3}{4} + \frac{1}{4} =$	$\frac{3}{4} - \frac{1}{4} =$	$\frac{3}{4} \times \frac{1}{4} =$	$\frac{3}{4} \div \frac{1}{4} =$
$\frac{2}{3} + \frac{1}{2} =$	$\frac{2}{3} - \frac{1}{2} =$	$\frac{2}{3} \times \frac{1}{2} =$	$\frac{2}{3} \div \frac{1}{2} =$
$\frac{3}{4} + \frac{2}{3} =$	$\frac{3}{4} - \frac{2}{3} =$	$\frac{3}{4} \times \frac{2}{3} =$	$\frac{3}{4} \div \frac{2}{3} =$

Mental Math

a.	**b.**	**c.**	**d.**
e.	**f.**	**g.**	**h.**

Problem Solving

Understand
What information am I given?
What am I asked to find or do?

Plan
How can I use the information I am given?
Which strategy should I try?

Solve
Did I follow the plan?
Did I show my work?
Did I write the answer?

Check
Did I use the correct information?
Did I do what was asked?
Is my answer reasonable?

© Houghton Mifflin Harcourt Publishing Company and Stephen Hake

Facts   Simplify.

$\frac{2}{3} + \frac{2}{3} =$	$\frac{2}{3} - \frac{1}{3} =$	$\frac{2}{3} \times \frac{2}{3} =$	$\frac{2}{3} \div \frac{2}{3} =$
$\frac{3}{4} + \frac{1}{4} =$	$\frac{3}{4} - \frac{1}{4} =$	$\frac{3}{4} \times \frac{1}{4} =$	$\frac{3}{4} \div \frac{1}{4} =$
$\frac{2}{3} + \frac{1}{2} =$	$\frac{2}{3} - \frac{1}{2} =$	$\frac{2}{3} \times \frac{1}{2} =$	$\frac{2}{3} \div \frac{1}{2} =$
$\frac{3}{4} + \frac{2}{3} =$	$\frac{3}{4} - \frac{2}{3} =$	$\frac{3}{4} \times \frac{2}{3} =$	$\frac{3}{4} \div \frac{2}{3} =$

Mental Math

a.	**b.**	**c.**	**d.**
e.	**f.**	**g.**	**h.**

Problem Solving

Understand

What information am I given?
What am I asked to find or do?

- -

Plan

How can I use the information I am given?
Which strategy should I try?

- -

Solve

Did I follow the plan?
Did I show my work?
Did I write the answer?

- -

Check

Did I use the correct information?
Did I do what was asked?
Is my answer reasonable?

© Houghton Mifflin Harcourt Publishing Company and Stephen Hake

Facts	Name each figure illustrated.

1.	2.	3.	4.
_____	_____	_____	_____

5.	6.	7.	8.
_____	_____	_____	_____

9.	10.	11.	12. A polygon whose sides are equal in length and whose angles are equal in measure is a _____.
_____	_____	_____	

Mental Math

a.	b.	c.	d.
e.	f.	g.	h.

Problem Solving

Understand
What information am I given?
What am I asked to find or do?

Plan
How can I use the information I am given?
Which strategy should I try?

Solve
Did I follow the plan?
Did I show my work?
Did I write the answer?

Check
Did I use the correct information?
Did I do what was asked?
Is my answer reasonable?

© Houghton Mifflin Harcourt Publishing Company and Stephen Hake

Facts Multiply.

9 × 8	8 × 2	10 × 10	6 × 3	4 × 2	5 × 5	9 × 9	6 × 4	9 × 6	7 × 3
9 × 3	6 × 5	0 × 0	7 × 6	8 × 8	7 × 4	5 × 3	9 × 7	2 × 2	8 × 6
7 × 7	6 × 2	4 × 3	8 × 5	4 × 4	3 × 2	n × 0	8 × 4	6 × 6	9 × 2
8 × 3	5 × 4	n × 1	7 × 2	9 × 5	8 × 7	3 × 3	9 × 4	5 × 2	7 × 5

Mental Math

a.	**b.**	**c.**	**d.**
e.	**f.**	**g.**	**h.**

Problem Solving

Understand

What information am I given?

What am I asked to find or do?

- -

Plan

How can I use the information I am given?

Which strategy should I try?

- -

Solve

Did I follow the plan?

Did I show my work?

Did I write the answer?

- -

Check

Did I use the correct information?

Did I do what was asked?

Is my answer reasonable?

© Houghton Mifflin Harcourt Publishing Company and Stephen Hake

Facts   Write the number that completes each equivalent measure.

1. 1 foot	= _____ inches
2. 1 yard	= _____ inches
3. 1 yard	= _____ feet
4. 1 mile	= _____ feet
5. 1 centimeter	= _____ millimeters
6. 1 meter	= _____ millimeters
7. 1 meter	= _____ centimeters
8. 1 kilometer	= _____ meters
9. 1 inch	= _____ centimeters
10. 1 pound	= _____ ounces
11. 1 ton	= _____ pounds
12. 1 gram	= _____ milligrams
13. 1 kilogram	= _____ grams
14. 1 metric ton	= _____ kilograms

15. 1 kilogram ≈ _____ pounds

16. 1 pint = _____ ounces

17. 1 pint = _____ cups

18. 1 quart = _____ pints

19. 1 gallon = _____ quarts

20. 1 liter = _____ milliliters

21–24. 1 milliliter of water has a volume of _____ and a mass of _____ .
One liter of water has a volume of _____ cm^3 and a mass of ___ kg.

25–26. Water freezes at ___ °F and ___ °C.

27–28. Water boils at ___ °F and ___ °C.

29–30. Normal body temperature is ___ °F and ___ °C.

Mental Math

a.	b.	c.	d.
e.	f.	g.	h.

Problem Solving

Understand
What information am I given?
What am I asked to find or do?

Plan
How can I use the information I am given?
Which strategy should I try?

Solve
Did I follow the plan?
Did I show my work?
Did I write the answer?

Check
Did I use the correct information?
Did I do what was asked?
Is my answer reasonable?

© Houghton Mifflin Harcourt Publishing Company and Stephen Hake

Facts Simplify.

$\frac{2}{3} + \frac{2}{3} =$	$\frac{2}{3} - \frac{1}{3} =$	$\frac{2}{3} \times \frac{2}{3} =$	$\frac{2}{3} \div \frac{2}{3} =$
$\frac{3}{4} + \frac{1}{4} =$	$\frac{3}{4} - \frac{1}{4} =$	$\frac{3}{4} \times \frac{1}{4} =$	$\frac{3}{4} \div \frac{1}{4} =$
$\frac{2}{3} + \frac{1}{2} =$	$\frac{2}{3} - \frac{1}{2} =$	$\frac{2}{3} \times \frac{1}{2} =$	$\frac{2}{3} \div \frac{1}{2} =$
$\frac{3}{4} + \frac{2}{3} =$	$\frac{3}{4} - \frac{2}{3} =$	$\frac{3}{4} \times \frac{2}{3} =$	$\frac{3}{4} \div \frac{2}{3} =$

Mental Math

a.	**b.**	**c.**	**d.**
e.	**f.**	**g.**	**h.**

Problem Solving

Understand

What information am I given?

What am I asked to find or do?

- -

Plan

How can I use the information I am given?

Which strategy should I try?

- -

Solve

Did I follow the plan?

Did I show my work?

Did I write the answer?

- -

Check

Did I use the correct information?

Did I do what was asked?

Is my answer reasonable?

© Houghton Mifflin Harcourt Publishing Company and Stephen Hake

Name _____ Time _____

Facts Write the number that completes each equivalent measure.

1. 1 foot	= _____	inches
2. 1 yard	= _____	inches
3. 1 yard	= _____	feet
4. 1 mile	= _____	feet
5. 1 centimeter	= _____	millimeters
6. 1 meter	= _____	millimeters
7. 1 meter	= _____	centimeters
8. 1 kilometer	= _____	meters
9. 1 inch	= _____	centimeters
10. 1 pound	= _____	ounces
11. 1 ton	= _____	pounds
12. 1 gram	= _____	milligrams
13. 1 kilogram	= _____	grams
14. 1 metric ton	= _____	kilograms

15. 1 kilogram	≈ _____	pounds
16. 1 pint	= _____	ounces
17. 1 pint	= _____	cups
18. 1 quart	= _____	pints
19. 1 gallon	= _____	quarts
20. 1 liter	= _____	milliliters

21–24. 1 milliliter of water has a volume of _____ and a mass of _____ .
One liter of water has a volume of _____ cm^3 and a mass of ___ kg.

25–26. Water freezes at ___ °F and ___ °C.

27–28. Water boils at ___ °F and ___ °C.

29–30. Normal body temperature is ___ °F and ___ °C.

Mental Math

a.	b.	c.	d.
e.	f.	g.	h.

Problem Solving

Understand
What information am I given?
What am I asked to find or do?

- -

Plan
How can I use the information I am given?
Which strategy should I try?

- -

Solve
Did I follow the plan?
Did I show my work?
Did I write the answer?

- -

Check
Did I use the correct information?
Did I do what was asked?
Is my answer reasonable?

© Houghton Mifflin Harcourt Publishing Company and Stephen Hake

Name _____ Time _____

Facts   Simplify.

$\frac{2}{3} + \frac{2}{3} =$	$\frac{2}{3} - \frac{1}{3} =$	$\frac{2}{3} \times \frac{2}{3} =$	$\frac{2}{3} \div \frac{2}{3} =$
$\frac{3}{4} + \frac{1}{4} =$	$\frac{3}{4} - \frac{1}{4} =$	$\frac{3}{4} \times \frac{1}{4} =$	$\frac{3}{4} \div \frac{1}{4} =$
$\frac{2}{3} + \frac{1}{2} =$	$\frac{2}{3} - \frac{1}{2} =$	$\frac{2}{3} \times \frac{1}{2} =$	$\frac{2}{3} \div \frac{1}{2} =$
$\frac{3}{4} + \frac{2}{3} =$	$\frac{3}{4} - \frac{2}{3} =$	$\frac{3}{4} \times \frac{2}{3} =$	$\frac{3}{4} \div \frac{2}{3} =$

Mental Math

a.	**b.**	**c.**	**d.**
e.	**f.**	**g.**	**h.**

Problem Solving

Understand

What information am I given?

What am I asked to find or do?

- -

Plan

How can I use the information I am given?

Which strategy should I try?

- -

Solve

Did I follow the plan?

Did I show my work?

Did I write the answer?

- -

Check

Did I use the correct information?

Did I do what was asked?

Is my answer reasonable?

© Houghton Mifflin Harcourt Publishing Company and Stephen Hake

Facts Write the number that completes each equivalent measure.

1. 1 foot	= _____	inches
2. 1 yard	= _____	inches
3. 1 yard	= _____	feet
4. 1 mile	= _____	feet
5. 1 centimeter	= _____	millimeters
6. 1 meter	= _____	millimeters
7. 1 meter	= _____	centimeters
8. 1 kilometer	= _____	meters
9. 1 inch	= _____	centimeters
10. 1 pound	= _____	ounces
11. 1 ton	= _____	pounds
12. 1 gram	= _____	milligrams
13. 1 kilogram	= _____	grams
14. 1 metric ton	= _____	kilograms

15. 1 kilogram	≈ _____	pounds
16. 1 pint	= _____	ounces
17. 1 pint	= _____	cups
18. 1 quart	= _____	pints
19. 1 gallon	= _____	quarts
20. 1 liter	= _____	milliliters

21–24. 1 milliliter of water has a volume of _____ and a mass of _____ .
One liter of water has a volume of _____ cm^3 and a mass of ___ kg.

25–26. Water freezes at ___ °F and ___ °C.

27–28. Water boils at ___ °F and ___ °C.

29–30. Normal body temperature is ___ °F and ___ °C.

Mental Math

a.	**b.**	**c.**	**d.**
e.	**f.**	**g.**	**h.**

Problem Solving

Understand
What information am I given?
What am I asked to find or do?

Plan
How can I use the information I am given?
Which strategy should I try?

Solve
Did I follow the plan?
Did I show my work?
Did I write the answer?

Check
Did I use the correct information?
Did I do what was asked?
Is my answer reasonable?

© Houghton Mifflin Harcourt Publishing Company and Stephen Hake

Facts   Simplify.

$\frac{2}{3} + \frac{2}{3} =$	$\frac{2}{3} - \frac{1}{3} =$	$\frac{2}{3} \times \frac{2}{3} =$	$\frac{2}{3} \div \frac{2}{3} =$
$\frac{3}{4} + \frac{1}{4} =$	$\frac{3}{4} - \frac{1}{4} =$	$\frac{3}{4} \times \frac{1}{4} =$	$\frac{3}{4} \div \frac{1}{4} =$
$\frac{2}{3} + \frac{1}{2} =$	$\frac{2}{3} - \frac{1}{2} =$	$\frac{2}{3} \times \frac{1}{2} =$	$\frac{2}{3} \div \frac{1}{2} =$
$\frac{3}{4} + \frac{2}{3} =$	$\frac{3}{4} - \frac{2}{3} =$	$\frac{3}{4} \times \frac{2}{3} =$	$\frac{3}{4} \div \frac{2}{3} =$

Mental Math

a.	b.	c.	d.
e.	f.	g.	h.

Problem Solving

Understand
What information am I given?
What am I asked to find or do?

Plan
How can I use the information I am given?
Which strategy should I try?

Solve
Did I follow the plan?
Did I show my work?
Did I write the answer?

Check
Did I use the correct information?
Did I do what was asked?
Is my answer reasonable?

© Houghton Mifflin Harcourt Publishing Company and Stephen Hake

Facts   Multiply.

9 × 8	8 × 2	10 × 10	6 × 3	4 × 2	5 × 5	9 × 9	6 × 4	9 × 6	7 × 3
9 × 3	6 × 5	0 × 0	7 × 6	8 × 8	7 × 4	5 × 3	9 × 7	2 × 2	8 × 6
7 × 7	6 × 2	4 × 3	8 × 5	4 × 4	3 × 2	*n* × 0	8 × 4	6 × 6	9 × 2
8 × 3	5 × 4	*n* × 1	7 × 2	9 × 5	8 × 7	3 × 3	9 × 4	5 × 2	7 × 5

Mental Math

a.	**b.**	**c.**	**d.**
e.	**f.**	**g.**	**h.**

Problem Solving

Understand

What information am I given?

What am I asked to find or do?

- -

Plan

How can I use the information I am given?

Which strategy should I try?

- -

Solve

Did I follow the plan?

Did I show my work?

Did I write the answer?

- -

Check

Did I use the correct information?

Did I do what was asked?

Is my answer reasonable?

© Houghton Mifflin Harcourt Publishing Company and Stephen Hake

Name _____ Time _____

Facts   Write the number that completes each equivalent measure.

1. 1 foot = _____ inches	15. 1 kilogram ≈ _____ pounds
2. 1 yard = _____ inches	16. 1 pint = _____ ounces
3. 1 yard = _____ feet	17. 1 pint = _____ cups
4. 1 mile = _____ feet	18. 1 quart = _____ pints
5. 1 centimeter = _____ millimeters	19. 1 gallon = _____ quarts
6. 1 meter = _____ millimeters	20. 1 liter = _____ milliliters
7. 1 meter = _____ centimeters	21–24. 1 milliliter of water has a volume of _____ and a mass of _____ .
8. 1 kilometer = _____ meters	One liter of water has a volume of _____ cm^3 and a mass of ___ kg.
9. 1 inch = _____ centimeters	
10. 1 pound = _____ ounces	25–26. Water freezes at ___ °F and ___ °C.
11. 1 ton = _____ pounds	27–28. Water boils at ___ °F and ___ °C.
12. 1 gram = _____ milligrams	29–30. Normal body temperature is ___ °F and ___ °C.
13. 1 kilogram = _____ grams	
14. 1 metric ton = _____ kilograms	

Mental Math

a.	b.	c.	d.
e.	f.	g.	h.

Problem Solving

Understand
What information am I given?
What am I asked to find or do?

Plan
How can I use the information I am given?
Which strategy should I try?

Solve
Did I follow the plan?
Did I show my work?
Did I write the answer?

Check
Did I use the correct information?
Did I do what was asked?
Is my answer reasonable?

Saxon Math Course 2

© Houghton Mifflin Harcourt Publishing Company and Stephen Hake

Facts Find the number that completes each proportion.

$\frac{3}{4} = \frac{a}{12}$	$\frac{3}{4} = \frac{12}{b}$	$\frac{c}{5} = \frac{12}{20}$	$\frac{2}{d} = \frac{12}{24}$	$\frac{8}{12} = \frac{4}{e}$
$\frac{f}{10} = \frac{10}{5}$	$\frac{5}{g} = \frac{25}{100}$	$\frac{10}{100} = \frac{5}{h}$	$\frac{8}{4} = \frac{j}{16}$	$\frac{24}{k} = \frac{8}{6}$
$\frac{9}{12} = \frac{36}{m}$	$\frac{50}{100} = \frac{w}{30}$	$\frac{3}{9} = \frac{5}{p}$	$\frac{q}{60} = \frac{15}{20}$	$\frac{2}{5} = \frac{r}{100}$

Mental Math

a.	**b.**	**c.**	**d.**
e.	**f.**	**g.**	**h.**

Problem Solving

Understand
What information am I given?
What am I asked to find or do?

Plan
How can I use the information I am given?
Which strategy should I try?

Solve
Did I follow the plan?
Did I show my work?
Did I write the answer?

Check
Did I use the correct information?
Did I do what was asked?
Is my answer reasonable?

© Houghton Mifflin Harcourt Publishing Company and Stephen Hake

Facts   Write the number that completes each equivalent measure.

1. 1 foot	= _____ inches	15. 1 kilogram ≈ _____ pounds	
2. 1 yard	= _____ inches	16. 1 pint	= _____ ounces
3. 1 yard	= _____ feet	17. 1 pint	= _____ cups
4. 1 mile	= _____ feet	18. 1 quart	= _____ pints
5. 1 centimeter	= _____ millimeters	19. 1 gallon	= _____ quarts
6. 1 meter	= _____ millimeters	20. 1 liter	= _____ milliliters
7. 1 meter	= _____ centimeters		
8. 1 kilometer	= _____ meters		
9. 1 inch	= _____ centimeters		

21–24. 1 milliliter of water has a volume of _____ and a mass of _____ .
One liter of water has a volume of _____ cm³ and a mass of ___ kg.

10. 1 pound	= _____ ounces
11. 1 ton	= _____ pounds
12. 1 gram	= _____ milligrams
13. 1 kilogram	= _____ grams
14. 1 metric ton	= _____ kilograms

25–26. Water freezes at ___ °F and ___ °C.

27–28. Water boils at ____ °F and ____ °C.

29–30. Normal body temperature is ____ °F and ___ °C.

Mental Math

a.	b.	c.	d.
e.	f.	g.	h.

Problem Solving

Understand
What information am I given?
What am I asked to find or do?

- -

Plan
How can I use the information I am given?
Which strategy should I try?

- -

Solve
Did I follow the plan?
Did I show my work?
Did I write the answer?

- -

Check
Did I use the correct information?
Did I do what was asked?
Is my answer reasonable?

© Houghton Mifflin Harcourt Publishing Company and Stephen Hake

Facts   Find the number that completes each proportion.

$\frac{3}{4} = \frac{a}{12}$	$\frac{3}{4} = \frac{12}{b}$	$\frac{c}{5} = \frac{12}{20}$	$\frac{2}{d} = \frac{12}{24}$	$\frac{8}{12} = \frac{4}{e}$
$\frac{f}{10} = \frac{10}{5}$	$\frac{5}{g} = \frac{25}{100}$	$\frac{10}{100} = \frac{5}{h}$	$\frac{8}{4} = \frac{j}{16}$	$\frac{24}{k} = \frac{8}{6}$
$\frac{9}{12} = \frac{36}{m}$	$\frac{50}{100} = \frac{w}{30}$	$\frac{3}{9} = \frac{5}{p}$	$\frac{q}{60} = \frac{15}{20}$	$\frac{2}{5} = \frac{r}{100}$

Mental Math

a.	b.	c.	d.
e.	f.	g.	h.

Problem Solving

Understand

What information am I given?

What am I asked to find or do?

- -

Plan

How can I use the information I am given?

Which strategy should I try?

- -

Solve

Did I follow the plan?

Did I show my work?

Did I write the answer?

- -

Check

Did I use the correct information?

Did I do what was asked?

Is my answer reasonable?

© Houghton Mifflin Harcourt Publishing Company and Stephen Hake

| Facts | Find the number that completes each proportion. |

$\frac{3}{4} = \frac{a}{12}$	$\frac{3}{4} = \frac{12}{b}$	$\frac{c}{5} = \frac{12}{20}$	$\frac{2}{d} = \frac{12}{24}$	$\frac{8}{12} = \frac{4}{e}$
$\frac{f}{10} = \frac{10}{5}$	$\frac{5}{g} = \frac{25}{100}$	$\frac{10}{100} = \frac{5}{h}$	$\frac{8}{4} = \frac{j}{16}$	$\frac{24}{k} = \frac{8}{6}$
$\frac{9}{12} = \frac{36}{m}$	$\frac{50}{100} = \frac{w}{30}$	$\frac{3}{9} = \frac{5}{p}$	$\frac{q}{60} = \frac{15}{20}$	$\frac{2}{5} = \frac{r}{100}$

Mental Math

a.	b.	c.	d.
e.	f.	g.	h.

Problem Solving

Understand
What information am I given?
What am I asked to find or do?

Plan
How can I use the information I am given?
Which strategy should I try?

Solve
Did I follow the plan?
Did I show my work?
Did I write the answer?

Check
Did I use the correct information?
Did I do what was asked?
Is my answer reasonable?

© Houghton Mifflin Harcourt Publishing Company and Stephen Hake

Facts   Find the number that completes each proportion.

$\frac{3}{4} = \frac{a}{12}$	$\frac{3}{4} = \frac{12}{b}$	$\frac{c}{5} = \frac{12}{20}$	$\frac{2}{d} = \frac{12}{24}$	$\frac{8}{12} = \frac{4}{e}$
$\frac{f}{10} = \frac{10}{5}$	$\frac{5}{g} = \frac{25}{100}$	$\frac{10}{100} = \frac{5}{h}$	$\frac{8}{4} = \frac{j}{16}$	$\frac{24}{k} = \frac{8}{6}$
$\frac{9}{12} = \frac{36}{m}$	$\frac{50}{100} = \frac{w}{30}$	$\frac{3}{9} = \frac{5}{p}$	$\frac{q}{60} = \frac{15}{20}$	$\frac{2}{5} = \frac{r}{100}$

Mental Math

a.	**b.**	**c.**	**d.**
e.	**f.**	**g.**	**h.**

Problem Solving

Understand

What information am I given?

What am I asked to find or do?

- -

Plan

How can I use the information I am given?

Which strategy should I try?

- -

Solve

Did I follow the plan?

Did I show my work?

Did I write the answer?

- -

Check

Did I use the correct information?

Did I do what was asked?

Is my answer reasonable?

© Houghton Mifflin Harcourt Publishing Company and Stephen Hake

Facts — Simplify.

0.8 + 0.4 =	0.8 − 0.4 =	0.8 × 0.4 =	0.8 ÷ 0.4 =
1.2 + 0.4 =	1.2 − 0.4 =	1.2 × 0.4 =	1.2 ÷ 0.4 =
6 + 0.3 =	6 − 0.3 =	6 × 0.3 =	6 ÷ 0.3 =
1.2 + 4 =	0.01 − 0.01 =	0.3 × 0.3 =	0.12 ÷ 4 =

Mental Math

a.	**b.**	**c.**	**d.**
e.	**f.**	**g.**	**h.**

Problem Solving

Understand
What information am I given?
What am I asked to find or do?

Plan
How can I use the information I am given?
Which strategy should I try?

Solve
Did I follow the plan?
Did I show my work?
Did I write the answer?

Check
Did I use the correct information?
Did I do what was asked?
Is my answer reasonable?

© Houghton Mifflin Harcourt Publishing Company and Stephen Hake

Name _____ Time _____

Facts   Simplify.

0.8 + 0.4 =	0.8 − 0.4 =	0.8 × 0.4 =	0.8 ÷ 0.4 =
1.2 + 0.4 =	1.2 − 0.4 =	1.2 × 0.4 =	1.2 ÷ 0.4 =
6 + 0.3 =	6 − 0.3 =	6 × 0.3 =	6 ÷ 0.3 =
1.2 + 4 =	0.01 − 0.01 =	0.3 × 0.3 =	0.12 ÷ 4 =

Mental Math

a.	b.	c.	d.
e.	f.	g.	h.

Problem Solving

Understand
What information am I given?
What am I asked to find or do?

- -

Plan
How can I use the information I am given?
Which strategy should I try?

- -

Solve
Did I follow the plan?
Did I show my work?
Did I write the answer?

- -

Check
Did I use the correct information?
Did I do what was asked?
Is my answer reasonable?

© Houghton Mifflin Harcourt Publishing Company and Stephen Hake

Facts   Find the number that completes each proportion.

$\frac{3}{4} = \frac{a}{12}$	$\frac{3}{4} = \frac{12}{b}$	$\frac{c}{5} = \frac{12}{20}$	$\frac{2}{d} = \frac{12}{24}$	$\frac{8}{12} = \frac{4}{e}$
$\frac{f}{10} = \frac{10}{5}$	$\frac{5}{g} = \frac{25}{100}$	$\frac{10}{100} = \frac{5}{h}$	$\frac{8}{4} = \frac{j}{16}$	$\frac{24}{k} = \frac{8}{6}$
$\frac{9}{12} = \frac{36}{m}$	$\frac{50}{100} = \frac{w}{30}$	$\frac{3}{9} = \frac{5}{p}$	$\frac{q}{60} = \frac{15}{20}$	$\frac{2}{5} = \frac{r}{100}$

Mental Math

a.	b.	c.	d.
e.	f.	g.	h.

Problem Solving

Understand
What information am I given?
What am I asked to find or do?

Plan
How can I use the information I am given?
Which strategy should I try?

Solve
Did I follow the plan?
Did I show my work?
Did I write the answer?

Check
Did I use the correct information?
Did I do what was asked?
Is my answer reasonable?

© Houghton Mifflin Harcourt Publishing Company and Stephen Hake

Saxon Math Course 2

Facts Simplify.			
0.8 + 0.4 =	0.8 − 0.4 =	0.8 × 0.4 =	0.8 ÷ 0.4 =
1.2 + 0.4 =	1.2 − 0.4 =	1.2 × 0.4 =	1.2 ÷ 0.4 =
6 + 0.3 =	6 − 0.3 =	6 × 0.3 =	6 ÷ 0.3 =
1.2 + 4 =	0.01 − 0.01 =	0.3 × 0.3 =	0.12 ÷ 4 =

Mental Math

a.	b.	c.	d.
e.	f.	g.	h.

Problem Solving

Understand

What information am I given?
What am I asked to find or do?

- -

Plan

How can I use the information I am given?
Which strategy should I try?

- -

Solve

Did I follow the plan?
Did I show my work?
Did I write the answer?

- -

Check

Did I use the correct information?
Did I do what was asked?
Is my answer reasonable?

© Houghton Mifflin Harcourt Publishing Company and Stephen Hake

Facts	Simplify each power or root.			
$\sqrt{100} =$	$\sqrt{16} =$	$\sqrt{81} =$	$\sqrt{4} =$	$\sqrt{144} =$
$\sqrt{64} =$	$\sqrt{49} =$	$\sqrt{25} =$	$\sqrt{9} =$	$\sqrt{36} =$
$8^2 =$	$5^2 =$	$3^2 =$	$12^2 =$	$10^2 =$
$7^2 =$	$2^3 =$	$3^3 =$	$10^3 =$	$5^3 =$

Mental Math			
a.	**b.**	**c.**	**d.**
e.	**f.**	**g.**	**h.**

Problem Solving

Understand

What information am I given?

What am I asked to find or do?

- -

Plan

How can I use the information I am given?

Which strategy should I try?

- -

Solve

Did I follow the plan?

Did I show my work?

Did I write the answer?

- -

Check

Did I use the correct information?

Did I do what was asked?

Is my answer reasonable?

© Houghton Mifflin Harcourt Publishing Company and Stephen Hake

Facts   Multiply.

9 × 8	8 × 2	10 × 10	6 × 3	4 × 2	5 × 5	9 × 9	6 × 4	9 × 6	7 × 3
9 × 3	6 × 5	0 × 0	7 × 6	8 × 8	7 × 4	5 × 3	9 × 7	2 × 2	8 × 6
7 × 7	6 × 2	4 × 3	8 × 5	4 × 4	3 × 2	n × 0	8 × 4	6 × 6	9 × 2
8 × 3	5 × 4	n × 1	7 × 2	9 × 5	8 × 7	3 × 3	9 × 4	5 × 2	7 × 5

Mental Math

a.	b.	c.	d.
e.	f.	g.	h.

Problem Solving

Understand

What information am I given?

What am I asked to find or do?

- -

Plan

How can I use the information I am given?

Which strategy should I try?

- -

Solve

Did I follow the plan?

Did I show my work?

Did I write the answer?

- -

Check

Did I use the correct information?

Did I do what was asked?

Is my answer reasonable?

© Houghton Mifflin Harcourt Publishing Company and Stephen Hake

Facts   Write the equivalent decimal and percent for each fraction.

Fraction	Decimal	Percent	Fraction	Decimal	Percent
$\frac{1}{2}$			$\frac{1}{8}$		
$\frac{1}{3}$			$\frac{1}{10}$		
$\frac{2}{3}$			$\frac{3}{10}$		
$\frac{1}{4}$			$\frac{9}{10}$		
$\frac{3}{4}$			$\frac{1}{100}$		
$\frac{1}{5}$			$1\frac{1}{2}$		

Mental Math

a.	b.	c.	d.
e.	f.	g.	h.

Problem Solving

Understand
What information am I given?
What am I asked to find or do?

Plan
How can I use the information I am given?
Which strategy should I try?

Solve
Did I follow the plan?
Did I show my work?
Did I write the answer?

Check
Did I use the correct information?
Did I do what was asked?
Is my answer reasonable?

Saxon Math Course 2

© Houghton Mifflin Harcourt Publishing Company and Stephen Hake

Facts	Simplify.		
0.8 + 0.4 =	0.8 − 0.4 =	0.8 × 0.4 =	0.8 ÷ 0.4 =
1.2 + 0.4 =	1.2 − 0.4 =	1.2 × 0.4 =	1.2 ÷ 0.4 =
6 + 0.3 =	6 − 0.3 =	6 × 0.3 =	6 ÷ 0.3 =
1.2 + 4 =	0.01 − 0.01 =	0.3 × 0.3 =	0.12 ÷ 4 =

Mental Math			
a.	**b.**	**c.**	**d.**
e.	**f.**	**g.**	**h.**

Problem Solving

Understand

What information am I given?
What am I asked to find or do?

- -

Plan

How can I use the information I am given?
Which strategy should I try?

- -

Solve

Did I follow the plan?
Did I show my work?
Did I write the answer?

- -

Check

Did I use the correct information?
Did I do what was asked?
Is my answer reasonable?

© Houghton Mifflin Harcourt Publishing Company and Stephen Hake

Facts   Write the equivalent decimal and percent for each fraction.

Fraction	Decimal	Percent	Fraction	Decimal	Percent
$\frac{1}{2}$			$\frac{1}{8}$		
$\frac{1}{3}$			$\frac{1}{10}$		
$\frac{2}{3}$			$\frac{3}{10}$		
$\frac{1}{4}$			$\frac{9}{10}$		
$\frac{3}{4}$			$\frac{1}{100}$		
$\frac{1}{5}$			$1\frac{1}{2}$		

Mental Math

a.	b.	c.	d.
e.	f.	g.	h.

Problem Solving

Understand

What information am I given?
What am I asked to find or do?

Plan

How can I use the information I am given?
Which strategy should I try?

Solve

Did I follow the plan?
Did I show my work?
Did I write the answer?

Check

Did I use the correct information?
Did I do what was asked?
Is my answer reasonable?

© Houghton Mifflin Harcourt Publishing Company and Stephen Hake

Facts Simplify each power or root.

$\sqrt{100} =$	$\sqrt{16} =$	$\sqrt{81} =$	$\sqrt{4} =$	$\sqrt{144} =$
$\sqrt{64} =$	$\sqrt{49} =$	$\sqrt{25} =$	$\sqrt{9} =$	$\sqrt{36} =$
$8^2 =$	$5^2 =$	$3^2 =$	$12^2 =$	$10^2 =$
$7^2 =$	$2^3 =$	$3^3 =$	$10^3 =$	$5^3 =$

Mental Math

a.	b.	c.	d.
e.	f.	g.	h.

Problem Solving

Understand
What information am I given?
What am I asked to find or do?

- -

Plan
How can I use the information I am given?
Which strategy should I try?

- -

Solve
Did I follow the plan?
Did I show my work?
Did I write the answer?

- -

Check
Did I use the correct information?
Did I do what was asked?
Is my answer reasonable?

© Houghton Mifflin Harcourt Publishing Company and Stephen Hake

Facts	Simplify each power or root.

$\sqrt{100} =$	$\sqrt{16} =$	$\sqrt{81} =$	$\sqrt{4} =$	$\sqrt{144} =$
$\sqrt{64} =$	$\sqrt{49} =$	$\sqrt{25} =$	$\sqrt{9} =$	$\sqrt{36} =$
$8^2 =$	$5^2 =$	$3^2 =$	$12^2 =$	$10^2 =$
$7^2 =$	$2^3 =$	$3^3 =$	$10^3 =$	$5^3 =$

Mental Math

a.	**b.**	**c.**	**d.**
e.	**f.**	**g.**	**h.**

Problem Solving

Understand
What information am I given?
What am I asked to find or do?

- -

Plan
How can I use the information I am given?
Which strategy should I try?

- -

Solve
Did I follow the plan?
Did I show my work?
Did I write the answer?

- -

Check
Did I use the correct information?
Did I do what was asked?
Is my answer reasonable?

© Houghton Mifflin Harcourt Publishing Company and Stephen Hake

Facts Write the equivalent decimal and percent for each fraction.

Fraction	Decimal	Percent	Fraction	Decimal	Percent
$\frac{1}{2}$			$\frac{1}{8}$		
$\frac{1}{3}$			$\frac{1}{10}$		
$\frac{2}{3}$			$\frac{3}{10}$		
$\frac{1}{4}$			$\frac{9}{10}$		
$\frac{3}{4}$			$\frac{1}{100}$		
$\frac{1}{5}$			$1\frac{1}{2}$		

Mental Math

a.	b.	c.	d.
e.	f.	g.	h.

Problem Solving

Understand
What information am I given?
What am I asked to find or do?

- -

Plan
How can I use the information I am given?
Which strategy should I try?

- -

Solve
Did I follow the plan?
Did I show my work?
Did I write the answer?

- -

Check
Did I use the correct information?
Did I do what was asked?
Is my answer reasonable?

© Houghton Mifflin Harcourt Publishing Company and Stephen Hake

Name _____ Time _____

Facts   Write the number for each conversion or factor.

1. 2 m = _____ cm

2. 1.5 km = _____ m

3. 2.54 cm = _____ mm

4. 125 cm = _____ m

5. 10 km = _____ m

6. 5000 m = _____ km

7. 50 cm = _____ m

8. 50 cm = _____ mm

9. 2 L = _____ mL

10. 250 mL = _____ L

11. 4 kg = _____ g

12. 2.5 g = _____ mg

13. 500 mg = _____ g

14. 0.5 kg = _____ g

15–16. Two liters of water have a volume of _____ cm³ and a mass of ___ kg.

	Prefix	Factor
17.	kilo-	
18.	hecto-	
19.	deka-	
	(unit)	
20.	deci-	
21.	centi-	
22.	milli-	

Mental Math

a.	b.	c.	d.
e.	f.	g.	h.

Problem Solving

Understand
What information am I given?
What am I asked to find or do?

Plan
How can I use the information I am given?
Which strategy should I try?

Solve
Did I follow the plan?
Did I show my work?
Did I write the answer?

Check
Did I use the correct information?
Did I do what was asked?
Is my answer reasonable?

© Houghton Mifflin Harcourt Publishing Company and Stephen Hake

Saxon Math Course 2

Facts   Write the equivalent decimal and percent for each fraction.

Fraction	Decimal	Percent	Fraction	Decimal	Percent
$\frac{1}{2}$			$\frac{1}{8}$		
$\frac{1}{3}$			$\frac{1}{10}$		
$\frac{2}{3}$			$\frac{3}{10}$		
$\frac{1}{4}$			$\frac{9}{10}$		
$\frac{3}{4}$			$\frac{1}{100}$		
$\frac{1}{5}$			$1\frac{1}{2}$		

Mental Math

a.	b.	c.	d.
e.	f.	g.	h.

Problem Solving

Understand

What information am I given?

What am I asked to find or do?

Plan

How can I use the information I am given?

Which strategy should I try?

Solve

Did I follow the plan?

Did I show my work?

Did I write the answer?

Check

Did I use the correct information?

Did I do what was asked?

Is my answer reasonable?

© Houghton Mifflin Harcourt Publishing Company and Stephen Hake

Facts   Write the number for each conversion or factor.

1. 2 m = _____ cm

2. 1.5 km = _____ m

3. 2.54 cm = _____ mm

4. 125 cm = _____ m

5. 10 km = _____ m

6. 5000 m = _____ km

7. 50 cm = _____ m

8. 50 cm = _____ mm

9. 2 L = _____ mL

10. 250 mL = _____ L

11. 4 kg = _____ g

12. 2.5 g = _____ mg

13. 500 mg = _____ g

14. 0.5 kg = _____ g

15–16. Two liters of water have a volume of _____ cm^3 and a mass of _____ kg.

	Prefix	Factor
17.	kilo-	
18.	hecto-	
19.	deka-	
	(unit)	
20.	deci-	
21.	centi-	
22.	milli-	

Mental Math

a.	b.	c.	d.
e.	f.	g.	h.

Problem Solving

Understand

What information am I given?

What am I asked to find or do?

- -

Plan

How can I use the information I am given?

Which strategy should I try?

- -

Solve

Did I follow the plan?

Did I show my work?

Did I write the answer?

- -

Check

Did I use the correct information?

Did I do what was asked?

Is my answer reasonable?

© Houghton Mifflin Harcourt Publishing Company and Stephen Hake

Facts Write the equivalent decimal and percent for each fraction.

Fraction	Decimal	Percent	Fraction	Decimal	Percent
$\frac{1}{2}$			$\frac{1}{8}$		
$\frac{1}{3}$			$\frac{1}{10}$		
$\frac{2}{3}$			$\frac{3}{10}$		
$\frac{1}{4}$			$\frac{9}{10}$		
$\frac{3}{4}$			$\frac{1}{100}$		
$\frac{1}{5}$			$1\frac{1}{2}$		

Mental Math

a.	b.	c.	d.
e.	f.	g.	h.

Problem Solving

Understand
What information am I given?
What am I asked to find or do?

Plan
How can I use the information I am given?
Which strategy should I try?

Solve
Did I follow the plan?
Did I show my work?
Did I write the answer?

Check
Did I use the correct information?
Did I do what was asked?
Is my answer reasonable?

© Houghton Mifflin Harcourt Publishing Company and Stephen Hake

Facts	Simplify. Reduce the answers if possible.		
$3 + 1\frac{2}{3} =$	$3 - 1\frac{2}{3} =$	$3 \times 1\frac{2}{3} =$	$3 \div 1\frac{2}{3} =$
$1\frac{2}{3} + 1\frac{1}{2} =$	$1\frac{2}{3} - 1\frac{1}{2} =$	$1\frac{2}{3} \times 1\frac{1}{2} =$	$1\frac{2}{3} \div 1\frac{1}{2} =$
$2\frac{1}{2} + 1\frac{2}{3} =$	$2\frac{1}{2} - 1\frac{2}{3} =$	$2\frac{1}{2} \times 1\frac{2}{3} =$	$2\frac{1}{2} \div 1\frac{2}{3} =$
$4\frac{1}{2} + 2\frac{1}{4} =$	$4\frac{1}{2} - 2\frac{1}{4} =$	$4\frac{1}{2} \times 2\frac{1}{4} =$	$4\frac{1}{2} \div 2\frac{1}{4} =$

Mental Math

a.	b.	c.	d.
e.	f.	g.	h.

Problem Solving

Understand

What information am I given?

What am I asked to find or do?

- -

Plan

How can I use the information I am given?

Which strategy should I try?

- -

Solve

Did I follow the plan?

Did I show my work?

Did I write the answer?

- -

Check

Did I use the correct information?

Did I do what was asked?

Is my answer reasonable?

© Houghton Mifflin Harcourt Publishing Company and Stephen Hake

Saxon Math Course 2

Facts Write the number for each conversion or factor.

1. 2 m = _____ cm	9. 2 L = _____ mL
2. 1.5 km = _____ m	10. 250 mL = _____ L
3. 2.54 cm = _____ mm	11. 4 kg = _____ g
4. 125 cm = _____ m	12. 2.5 g = _____ mg
5. 10 km = _____ m	13. 500 mg = _____ g
6. 5000 m = _____ km	14. 0.5 kg = _____ g
7. 50 cm = _____ m	15–16. Two liters of water have
8. 50 cm = _____ mm	a volume of _____ cm³ and a mass of _____ kg.

	Prefix	Factor
17.	kilo-	
18.	hecto-	
19.	deka-	
	(unit)	
20.	deci-	
21.	centi-	
22.	milli-	

Mental Math

a.	b.	c.	d.
e.	f.	g.	h.

Problem Solving

Understand
What information am I given?
What am I asked to find or do?

- -

Plan
How can I use the information I am given?
Which strategy should I try?

- -

Solve
Did I follow the plan?
Did I show my work?
Did I write the answer?

- -

Check
Did I use the correct information?
Did I do what was asked?
Is my answer reasonable?

© Houghton Mifflin Harcourt Publishing Company and Stephen Hake

Facts — Simplify. Reduce the answers if possible.

$3 + 1\frac{2}{3} =$	$3 - 1\frac{2}{3} =$	$3 \times 1\frac{2}{3} =$	$3 \div 1\frac{2}{3} =$
$1\frac{2}{3} + 1\frac{1}{2} =$	$1\frac{2}{3} - 1\frac{1}{2} =$	$1\frac{2}{3} \times 1\frac{1}{2} =$	$1\frac{2}{3} \div 1\frac{1}{2} =$
$2\frac{1}{2} + 1\frac{2}{3} =$	$2\frac{1}{2} - 1\frac{2}{3} =$	$2\frac{1}{2} \times 1\frac{2}{3} =$	$2\frac{1}{2} \div 1\frac{2}{3} =$
$4\frac{1}{2} + 2\frac{1}{4} =$	$4\frac{1}{2} - 2\frac{1}{4} =$	$4\frac{1}{2} \times 2\frac{1}{4} =$	$4\frac{1}{2} \div 2\frac{1}{4} =$

Mental Math

a.	b.	c.	d.
e.	**f.**	**g.**	**h.**

Problem Solving

Understand

What information am I given?

What am I asked to find or do?

- -

Plan

How can I use the information I am given?

Which strategy should I try?

- -

Solve

Did I follow the plan?

Did I show my work?

Did I write the answer?

- -

Check

Did I use the correct information?

Did I do what was asked?

Is my answer reasonable?

© Houghton Mifflin Harcourt Publishing Company and Stephen Hake

Facts Write the number for each conversion or factor.

1. 2 m = _____ cm	9. 2 L = _____ mL		**Prefix**	**Factor**
2. 1.5 km = _____ m	10. 250 mL = _____ L	17.	kilo-	
3. 2.54 cm = _____ mm	11. 4 kg = _____ g	18.	hecto-	
4. 125 cm = _____ m	12. 2.5 g = _____ mg	19.	deka-	
5. 10 km = _____ m	13. 500 mg = _____ g		(unit)	
6. 5000 m = _____ km	14. 0.5 kg = _____ g	20.	deci-	
7. 50 cm = _____ m	15–16. Two liters of water have a volume of _____ cm³ and a mass of _____ kg.	21.	centi-	
8. 50 cm = _____ mm		22.	milli-	

Mental Math

a.	b.	c.	d.
e.	f.	g.	h.

Problem Solving

Understand
What information am I given?
What am I asked to find or do?

- -

Plan
How can I use the information I am given?
Which strategy should I try?

- -

Solve
Did I follow the plan?
Did I show my work?
Did I write the answer?

- -

Check
Did I use the correct information?
Did I do what was asked?
Is my answer reasonable?

© Houghton Mifflin Harcourt Publishing Company and Stephen Hake

Facts	Simplify. Reduce the answers if possible.		
$3 + 1\frac{2}{3} =$	$3 - 1\frac{2}{3} =$	$3 \times 1\frac{2}{3} =$	$3 \div 1\frac{2}{3} =$
$1\frac{2}{3} + 1\frac{1}{2} =$	$1\frac{2}{3} - 1\frac{1}{2} =$	$1\frac{2}{3} \times 1\frac{1}{2} =$	$1\frac{2}{3} \div 1\frac{1}{2} =$
$2\frac{1}{2} + 1\frac{2}{3} =$	$2\frac{1}{2} - 1\frac{2}{3} =$	$2\frac{1}{2} \times 1\frac{2}{3} =$	$2\frac{1}{2} \div 1\frac{2}{3} =$
$4\frac{1}{2} + 2\frac{1}{4} =$	$4\frac{1}{2} - 2\frac{1}{4} =$	$4\frac{1}{2} \times 2\frac{1}{4} =$	$4\frac{1}{2} \div 2\frac{1}{4} =$

Mental Math			
a.	**b.**	**c.**	**d.**
e.	**f.**	**g.**	**h.**

Problem Solving

Understand
What information am I given?
What am I asked to find or do?

Plan
How can I use the information I am given?
Which strategy should I try?

Solve
Did I follow the plan?
Did I show my work?
Did I write the answer?

Check
Did I use the correct information?
Did I do what was asked?
Is my answer reasonable?

© Houghton Mifflin Harcourt Publishing Company and Stephen Hake

Saxon Math Course 2

Facts   Write the number for each conversion or factor.

1. 2 m	= _____ cm	9. 2 L	= _____ mL		
2. 1.5 km	= _____ m	10. 250 mL	= _____ L		
3. 2.54 cm	= _____ mm	11. 4 kg	= _____ g		
4. 125 cm	= _____ m	12. 2.5 g	= _____ mg		
5. 10 km	= _____ m	13. 500 mg	= _____ g		
6. 5000 m	= _____ km	14. 0.5 kg	= _____ g		
7. 50 cm	= _____ m				
8. 50 cm	= _____ mm				

15–16. Two liters of water have a volume of _____ cm³ and a mass of _____ kg.

	Prefix	Factor
17.	kilo-	
18.	hecto-	
19.	deka-	
	(unit)	
20.	deci-	
21.	centi-	
22.	milli-	

Mental Math

a.	b.	c.	d.
e.	f.	g.	h.

Problem Solving

Understand
What information am I given?
What am I asked to find or do?

- -

Plan
How can I use the information I am given?
Which strategy should I try?

- -

Solve
Did I follow the plan?
Did I show my work?
Did I write the answer?

- -

Check
Did I use the correct information?
Did I do what was asked?
Is my answer reasonable?

© Houghton Mifflin Harcourt Publishing Company and Stephen Hake

Facts — Simplify. Reduce the answers if possible.

$3 + 1\frac{2}{3} =$	$3 - 1\frac{2}{3} =$	$3 \times 1\frac{2}{3} =$	$3 \div 1\frac{2}{3} =$
$1\frac{2}{3} + 1\frac{1}{2} =$	$1\frac{2}{3} - 1\frac{1}{2} =$	$1\frac{2}{3} \times 1\frac{1}{2} =$	$1\frac{2}{3} \div 1\frac{1}{2} =$
$2\frac{1}{2} + 1\frac{2}{3} =$	$2\frac{1}{2} - 1\frac{2}{3} =$	$2\frac{1}{2} \times 1\frac{2}{3} =$	$2\frac{1}{2} \div 1\frac{2}{3} =$
$4\frac{1}{2} + 2\frac{1}{4} =$	$4\frac{1}{2} - 2\frac{1}{4} =$	$4\frac{1}{2} \times 2\frac{1}{4} =$	$4\frac{1}{2} \div 2\frac{1}{4} =$

Mental Math

a.	b.	c.	d.
e.	**f.**	**g.**	**h.**

Problem Solving

Understand

What information am I given?

What am I asked to find or do?

- -

Plan

How can I use the information I am given?

Which strategy should I try?

- -

Solve

Did I follow the plan?

Did I show my work?

Did I write the answer?

- -

Check

Did I use the correct information?

Did I do what was asked?

Is my answer reasonable?

© Houghton Mifflin Harcourt Publishing Company and Stephen Hake

Name _____ Time _____

Facts Select from the words below to describe each figure.

1.	2.	3.	4.
_____	_____	_____	_____
_____	_____	_____	_____

5.	6.	7.	8.
_____	_____	_____	_____
_____	_____	_____	_____

kite	rectangle	isosceles triangle	right triangle
trapezoid	rhombus	scalene triangle	acute triangle
parallelogram	square	equilateral triangle	obtuse triangle

Mental Math

a.	b.	c.	d.
e.	f.	g.	h.

Problem Solving

Understand
What information am I given?
What am I asked to find or do?

- -

Plan
How can I use the information I am given?
Which strategy should I try?

- -

Solve
Did I follow the plan?
Did I show my work?
Did I write the answer?

- -

Check
Did I use the correct information?
Did I do what was asked?
Is my answer reasonable?

© Houghton Mifflin Harcourt Publishing Company and Stephen Hake

Saxon Math Course 2

Facts   Simplify. Reduce the answers if possible.

$3 + 1\frac{2}{3} =$	$3 - 1\frac{2}{3} =$	$3 \times 1\frac{2}{3} =$	$3 \div 1\frac{2}{3} =$
$1\frac{2}{3} + 1\frac{1}{2} =$	$1\frac{2}{3} - 1\frac{1}{2} =$	$1\frac{2}{3} \times 1\frac{1}{2} =$	$1\frac{2}{3} \div 1\frac{1}{2} =$
$2\frac{1}{2} + 1\frac{2}{3} =$	$2\frac{1}{2} - 1\frac{2}{3} =$	$2\frac{1}{2} \times 1\frac{2}{3} =$	$2\frac{1}{2} \div 1\frac{2}{3} =$
$4\frac{1}{2} + 2\frac{1}{4} =$	$4\frac{1}{2} - 2\frac{1}{4} =$	$4\frac{1}{2} \times 2\frac{1}{4} =$	$4\frac{1}{2} \div 2\frac{1}{4} =$

Mental Math

a.	**b.**	**c.**	**d.**
e.	**f.**	**g.**	**h.**

Problem Solving

Understand
What information am I given?
What am I asked to find or do?

- -

Plan
How can I use the information I am given?
Which strategy should I try?

- -

Solve
Did I follow the plan?
Did I show my work?
Did I write the answer?

- -

Check
Did I use the correct information?
Did I do what was asked?
Is my answer reasonable?

© Houghton Mifflin Harcourt Publishing Company and Stephen Hake

Facts Select from the words below to describe each figure.

1.	2.	3.	4.
_____	_____	_____	_____ _____ _____

5.	6.	7.	8.
_____	_____	_____	_____

kite	rectangle	isosceles triangle	right triangle
trapezoid	rhombus	scalene triangle	acute triangle
parallelogram	square	equilateral triangle	obtuse triangle

Mental Math

a.	b.	c.	d.
e.	f.	g.	h.

Problem Solving

Understand
What information am I given?
What am I asked to find or do?

- -

Plan
How can I use the information I am given?
Which strategy should I try?

- -

Solve
Did I follow the plan?
Did I show my work?
Did I write the answer?

- -

Check
Did I use the correct information?
Did I do what was asked?
Is my answer reasonable?

© Houghton Mifflin Harcourt Publishing Company and Stephen Hake

Facts	Simplify. Reduce the answers if possible.		
$3 + 1\frac{2}{3} =$	$3 - 1\frac{2}{3} =$	$3 \times 1\frac{2}{3} =$	$3 \div 1\frac{2}{3} =$
$1\frac{2}{3} + 1\frac{1}{2} =$	$1\frac{2}{3} - 1\frac{1}{2} =$	$1\frac{2}{3} \times 1\frac{1}{2} =$	$1\frac{2}{3} \div 1\frac{1}{2} =$
$2\frac{1}{2} + 1\frac{2}{3} =$	$2\frac{1}{2} - 1\frac{2}{3} =$	$2\frac{1}{2} \times 1\frac{2}{3} =$	$2\frac{1}{2} \div 1\frac{2}{3} =$
$4\frac{1}{2} + 2\frac{1}{4} =$	$4\frac{1}{2} - 2\frac{1}{4} =$	$4\frac{1}{2} \times 2\frac{1}{4} =$	$4\frac{1}{2} \div 2\frac{1}{4} =$

Mental Math

a.	b.	c.	d.
e.	f.	g.	h.

Problem Solving

Understand
What information am I given?
What am I asked to find or do?

- -

Plan
How can I use the information I am given?
Which strategy should I try?

- -

Solve
Did I follow the plan?
Did I show my work?
Did I write the answer?

- -

Check
Did I use the correct information?
Did I do what was asked?
Is my answer reasonable?

© Houghton Mifflin Harcourt Publishing Company and Stephen Hake

Facts Select from the words below to describe each figure.

1.	2.	3.	4.
_____ _____ _____	_____ _____	_____ _____	_____ _____ _____

5.	6.	7.	8.
_____ _____	_____ _____	_____ _____	_____ _____

kite	rectangle	isosceles triangle	right triangle
trapezoid	rhombus	scalene triangle	acute triangle
parallelogram	square	equilateral triangle	obtuse triangle

Mental Math

a.	b.	c.	d.
e.	f.	g.	h.

Problem Solving

Understand
What information am I given?
What am I asked to find or do?

- -

Plan
How can I use the information I am given?
Which strategy should I try?

- -

Solve
Did I follow the plan?
Did I show my work?
Did I write the answer?

- -

Check
Did I use the correct information?
Did I do what was asked?
Is my answer reasonable?

© Houghton Mifflin Harcourt Publishing Company and Stephen Hake

Facts	Simplify.		
$(-8) + (-2) =$	$(-8) - (-2) =$	$(-8)(-2) =$	$\dfrac{-8}{-2} =$
$(-9) + (+3) =$	$(-9) - (+3) =$	$(-9)(+3) =$	$\dfrac{-9}{+3} =$
$12 + (-2) =$	$12 - (-2) =$	$(12)(-2) =$	$\dfrac{12}{-2} =$
$(-4) + (-3) + (-2) =$	$(-4) - (-3) - (-2) =$	$(-4)(-3)(-2) =$	$\dfrac{(-4)(-3)}{(-2)} =$

Mental Math

a.	b.	c.	d.
e.	f.	g.	h.

Problem Solving

Understand
What information am I given?
What am I asked to find or do?

Plan
How can I use the information I am given?
Which strategy should I try?

Solve
Did I follow the plan?
Did I show my work?
Did I write the answer?

Check
Did I use the correct information?
Did I do what was asked?
Is my answer reasonable?

© Houghton Mifflin Harcourt Publishing Company and Stephen Hake

Saxon Math Course 2

Facts   Simplify.

$(-8) + (-2) =$	$(-8) - (-2) =$	$(-8)(-2) =$	$\dfrac{-8}{-2} =$
$(-9) + (+3) =$	$(-9) - (+3) =$	$(-9)(+3) =$	$\dfrac{-9}{+3} =$
$12 + (-2) =$	$12 - (-2) =$	$(12)(-2) =$	$\dfrac{12}{-2} =$
$(-4) + (-3) + (-2) =$	$(-4) - (-3) - (-2) =$	$(-4)(-3)(-2) =$	$\dfrac{(-4)(-3)}{(-2)} =$

Mental Math

a.	**b.**	**c.**	**d.**
e.	**f.**	**g.**	**h.**

Problem Solving

Understand

What information am I given?

What am I asked to find or do?

Plan

How can I use the information I am given?

Which strategy should I try?

Solve

Did I follow the plan?

Did I show my work?

Did I write the answer?

Check

Did I use the correct information?

Did I do what was asked?

Is my answer reasonable?

© Houghton Mifflin Harcourt Publishing Company and Stephen Hake

Facts Select from the words below to describe each figure.

1.	2.	3.	4.
_____ _____ _____	_____ _____	_____ _____	_____ _____ _____

5.	6.	7.	8.
_____	_____	_____	_____

kite	rectangle	isosceles triangle	right triangle
trapezoid	rhombus	scalene triangle	acute triangle
parallelogram	square	equilateral triangle	obtuse triangle

Mental Math

a.	b.	c.	d.
e.	**f.**	**g.**	**h.**

Problem Solving

Understand

What information am I given?

What am I asked to find or do?

- -

Plan

How can I use the information I am given?

Which strategy should I try?

- -

Solve

Did I follow the plan?

Did I show my work?

Did I write the answer?

- -

Check

Did I use the correct information?

Did I do what was asked?

Is my answer reasonable?

© Houghton Mifflin Harcourt Publishing Company and Stephen Hake

Facts   Simplify.

(−8) + (−2) =	(−8) − (−2) =	(−8)(−2) =	$\frac{-8}{-2} =$
(−9) + (+3) =	(−9) − (+3) =	(−9)(+3) =	$\frac{-9}{+3} =$
12 + (−2) =	12 − (−2) =	(12)(−2) =	$\frac{12}{-2} =$
(−4) + (−3) + (−2) =	(−4) − (−3) − (−2) =	(−4)(−3)(−2) =	$\frac{(-4)(-3)}{(-2)} =$

Mental Math

a.	b.	c.	d.
e.	f.	g.	h.

Problem Solving

Understand

What information am I given?
What am I asked to find or do?

Plan

How can I use the information I am given?
Which strategy should I try?

Solve

Did I follow the plan?
Did I show my work?
Did I write the answer?

Check

Did I use the correct information?
Did I do what was asked?
Is my answer reasonable?

© Houghton Mifflin Harcourt Publishing Company and Stephen Hake

Facts   Select from the words below to describe each figure.

1.

_____
_____
_____

2.

_____
_____
_____

3.

_____
_____
_____

4.

_____
_____
_____

5.

_____
_____
_____

6.

_____
_____
_____

7.

_____
_____
_____

8.

_____
_____
_____

kite	rectangle	isosceles triangle	right triangle
trapezoid	rhombus	scalene triangle	acute triangle
parallelogram	square	equilateral triangle	obtuse triangle

Mental Math

a.	b.	c.	d.
e.	f.	g.	h.

Problem Solving

Understand
What information am I given?
What am I asked to find or do?

- -

Plan
How can I use the information I am given?
Which strategy should I try?

- -

Solve
Did I follow the plan?
Did I show my work?
Did I write the answer?

- -

Check
Did I use the correct information?
Did I do what was asked?
Is my answer reasonable?

© Houghton Mifflin Harcourt Publishing Company and Stephen Hake

Facts   Simplify.

$(-8) + (-2) =$	$(-8) - (-2) =$	$(-8)(-2) =$	$\dfrac{-8}{-2} =$
$(-9) + (+3) =$	$(-9) - (+3) =$	$(-9)(+3) =$	$\dfrac{-9}{+3} =$
$12 + (-2) =$	$12 - (-2) =$	$(12)(-2) =$	$\dfrac{12}{-2} =$
$(-4) + (-3) + (-2) =$	$(-4) - (-3) - (-2) =$	$(-4)(-3)(-2) =$	$\dfrac{(-4)(-3)}{(-2)} =$

Mental Math

a.	b.	c.	d.
e.	f.	g.	h.

Problem Solving

Understand

What information am I given?

What am I asked to find or do?

Plan

How can I use the information I am given?

Which strategy should I try?

Solve

Did I follow the plan?

Did I show my work?

Did I write the answer?

Check

Did I use the correct information?

Did I do what was asked?

Is my answer reasonable?

© Houghton Mifflin Harcourt Publishing Company and Stephen Hake

Facts   Write the equivalent decimal and fraction for each percent.

Percent	Decimal	Fraction	Percent	Decimal	Fraction
10%			$33\frac{1}{3}\%$		
90%			20%		
5%			75%		
$12\frac{1}{2}\%$			$66\frac{2}{3}\%$		
50%			1%		
25%			250%		

Mental Math

a.	**b.**	**c.**	**d.**
e.	**f.**	**g.**	**h.**

Problem Solving

Understand
What information am I given?
What am I asked to find or do?

Plan
How can I use the information I am given?
Which strategy should I try?

Solve
Did I follow the plan?
Did I show my work?
Did I write the answer?

Check
Did I use the correct information?
Did I do what was asked?
Is my answer reasonable?

© Houghton Mifflin Harcourt Publishing Company and Stephen Hake

Facts   Find the area of each figure. Angles that look like right angles are right angles.

1. 10 cm 10 cm (square) _____	2. 8 in. 4 in. (rectangle) _____

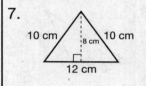

3. 6 cm / 4 cm / 5 cm
_____

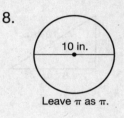

4. 7 cm / 5 cm / 4 cm / 10 cm
_____

5. 6 cm / 10 cm / 8 cm _____	6. 10 in. / 6 in. / 6 in. _____

7. 10 cm / 8 cm / 10 cm / 12 cm
_____

8. 10 in. (circle)
Leave π as π.
_____

Mental Math

a.	b.	c.	d.
e.	f.	g.	h.

Problem Solving

Understand
What information am I given?
What am I asked to find or do?

- -

Plan
How can I use the information I am given?
Which strategy should I try?

- -

Solve
Did I follow the plan?
Did I show my work?
Did I write the answer?

- -

Check
Did I use the correct information?
Did I do what was asked?
Is my answer reasonable?

© Houghton Mifflin Harcourt Publishing Company and Stephen Hake

Facts | Find the area of each figure. Angles that look like right angles are right angles.

1.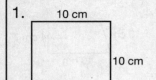
10 cm
10 cm

_____

2.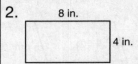
8 in.
4 in.

_____

3.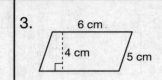
6 cm
4 cm
5 cm

_____

4.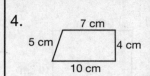
7 cm
5 cm
4 cm
10 cm

_____

5.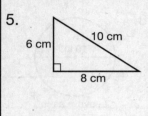
6 cm
10 cm
8 cm

_____

6.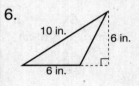
10 in.
6 in.
6 in.

_____

7.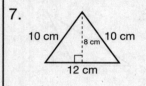
10 cm
8 cm
10 cm
12 cm

_____

8.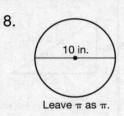
10 in.

Leave π as π.

_____

Mental Math

a.	b.	c.	d.
e.	f.	g.	h.

Problem Solving

Understand
What information am I given?
What am I asked to find or do?

- -

Plan
How can I use the information I am given?
Which strategy should I try?

- -

Solve
Did I follow the plan?
Did I show my work?
Did I write the answer?

- -

Check
Did I use the correct information?
Did I do what was asked?
Is my answer reasonable?

© Houghton Mifflin Harcourt Publishing Company and Stephen Hake

Saxon Math Course 2

Facts   Simplify.

$(-8) + (-2) =$	$(-8) - (-2) =$	$(-8)(-2) =$	$\dfrac{-8}{-2} =$
$(-9) + (+3) =$	$(-9) - (+3) =$	$(-9)(+3) =$	$\dfrac{-9}{+3} =$
$12 + (-2) =$	$12 - (-2) =$	$(12)(-2) =$	$\dfrac{12}{-2} =$
$(-4) + (-3) + (-2) =$	$(-4) - (-3) - (-2) =$	$(-4)(-3)(-2) =$	$\dfrac{(-4)(-3)}{(-2)} =$

Mental Math

a.	b.	c.	d.
e.	f.	g.	h.

Problem Solving

Understand
What information am I given?
What am I asked to find or do?

- -

Plan
How can I use the information I am given?
Which strategy should I try?

- -

Solve
Did I follow the plan?
Did I show my work?
Did I write the answer?

- -

Check
Did I use the correct information?
Did I do what was asked?
Is my answer reasonable?

© Houghton Mifflin Harcourt Publishing Company and Stephen Hake

Facts   Write each number in scientific notation.

186,000 =	0.0005 =	30,500,000 =
2.5 billion =	12 million =	$\dfrac{1}{1,000,000} =$

Write each number in standard form.

$1 \times 10^6 =$	$1 \times 10^{-6} =$	$2.4 \times 10^4 =$
$5 \times 10^{-4} =$	$4.75 \times 10^5 =$	$2.5 \times 10^{-3} =$

Mental Math

a.	b.	c.	d.
e.	f.	g.	h.

Problem Solving

Understand
What information am I given?
What am I asked to find or do?

- -

Plan
How can I use the information I am given?
Which strategy should I try?

- -

Solve
Did I follow the plan?
Did I show my work?
Did I write the answer?

- -

Check
Did I use the correct information?
Did I do what was asked?
Is my answer reasonable?

© Houghton Mifflin Harcourt Publishing Company and Stephen Hake

Name _____ Time _____

Facts Find the area of each figure. Angles that look like right angles are right angles.

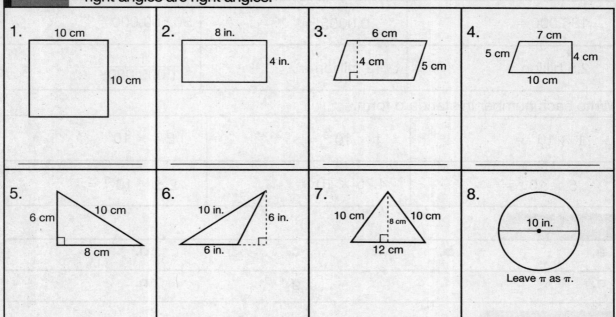

1. 10 cm / 10 cm

2. 8 in. / 4 in.

3. 6 cm / 4 cm / 5 cm

4. 7 cm / 5 cm / 4 cm / 10 cm

5. 6 cm / 10 cm / 8 cm

6. 10 in. / 6 in. / 6 in.

7. 10 cm / 8 cm / 10 cm / 12 cm

8. 10 in. / Leave π as π.

Mental Math

a.	b.	c.	d.
e.	f.	g.	h.

Problem Solving

Understand

What information am I given?

What am I asked to find or do?

- -

Plan

How can I use the information I am given?

Which strategy should I try?

- -

Solve

Did I follow the plan?

Did I show my work?

Did I write the answer?

- -

Check

Did I use the correct information?

Did I do what was asked?

Is my answer reasonable?

© Houghton Mifflin Harcourt Publishing Company and Stephen Hake

Facts	Write each number in scientific notation.	
186,000 =	0.0005 =	30,500,000 =
2.5 billion =	12 million =	$\dfrac{1}{1,000,000}=$

Write each number in standard form.

$1 \times 10^6 =$	$1 \times 10^{-6} =$	$2.4 \times 10^4 =$
$5 \times 10^{-4} =$	$4.75 \times 10^5 =$	$2.5 \times 10^{-3} =$

Mental Math			
a.	**b.**	**c.**	**d.**
e.	**f.**	**g.**	**h.**

Problem Solving

Understand
What information am I given?
What am I asked to find or do?

- -

Plan
How can I use the information I am given?
Which strategy should I try?

- -

Solve
Did I follow the plan?
Did I show my work?
Did I write the answer?

- -

Check
Did I use the correct information?
Did I do what was asked?
Is my answer reasonable?

© Houghton Mifflin Harcourt Publishing Company and Stephen Hake

© Houghton Mifflin Harcourt Publishing Company and Stephen Hake

Facts   Find the area of each figure. Angles that look like right angles are right angles.

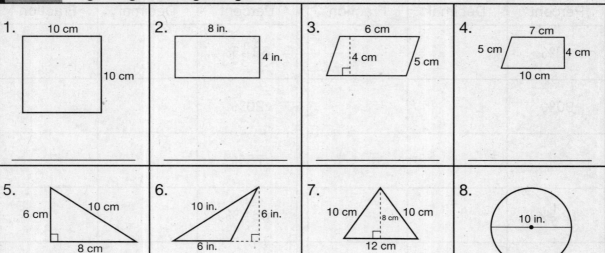

1. 10 cm / 10 cm _____	2. 8 in. / 4 in. _____
3. 6 cm / 4 cm / 5 cm _____	4. 7 cm / 5 cm / 4 cm / 10 cm _____

5. 6 cm / 10 cm / 8 cm _____	6. 10 in. / 6 in. / 6 in. _____
7. 10 cm / 8 cm / 10 cm / 12 cm _____	8. 10 in. / Leave π as π. _____

Mental Math

a.	b.	c.	d.
e.	f.	g.	h.

Problem Solving

Understand
What information am I given?
What am I asked to find or do?

- -

Plan
How can I use the information I am given?
Which strategy should I try?

- -

Solve
Did I follow the plan?
Did I show my work?
Did I write the answer?

- -

Check
Did I use the correct information?
Did I do what was asked?
Is my answer reasonable?

Facts Write the equivalent decimal and fraction for each percent.

Percent	Decimal	Fraction	Percent	Decimal	Fraction
10%			$33\frac{1}{3}$%		
90%			20%		
5%			75%		
$12\frac{1}{2}$%			$66\frac{2}{3}$%		
50%			1%		
25%			250%		

Mental Math

a.	**b.**	**c.**	**d.**
e.	**f.**	**g.**	**h.**

Problem Solving

Understand
What information am I given?
What am I asked to find or do?

Plan
How can I use the information I am given?
Which strategy should I try?

Solve
Did I follow the plan?
Did I show my work?
Did I write the answer?

Check
Did I use the correct information?
Did I do what was asked?
Is my answer reasonable?

© Houghton Mifflin Harcourt Publishing Company and Stephen Hake

Facts   Write each number in scientific notation.

186,000 =	0.0005 =	30,500,000 =
2.5 billion =	12 million =	$\dfrac{1}{1,000,000}$ =

Write each number in standard form.

1×10^6 =	1×10^{-6} =	2.4×10^4 =
5×10^{-4} =	4.75×10^5 =	2.5×10^{-3} =

Mental Math

a.	b.	c.	d.
e.	f.	g.	h.

Problem Solving

Understand
What information am I given?
What am I asked to find or do?

- -

Plan
How can I use the information I am given?
Which strategy should I try?

- -

Solve
Did I follow the plan?
Did I show my work?
Did I write the answer?

- -

Check
Did I use the correct information?
Did I do what was asked?
Is my answer reasonable?

© Houghton Mifflin Harcourt Publishing Company and Stephen Hake

Facts Simplify.

$6 + 6 \times 6 - 6 \div 6 =$	$3^2 + \sqrt{4} + 5(6) - 7 + 8 =$
$4 + 2(3 + 5) - 6 \div 2 =$	$2 + 2[3 + 4(7 - 5)] =$
$\sqrt{1^3 + 2^3 + 3^3} =$	$\dfrac{4 + 3(7 - 5)}{6 - (5 - 4)} =$
$(-3)(-3) + (-3) - (-3) =$	$\dfrac{3(-3) - (-3)(-3)}{(-3) - (3)(-3)} =$

Mental Math

a.	b.	c.	d.
e.	f.	g.	h.

Problem Solving

Understand

What information am I given?
What am I asked to find or do?

- -

Plan

How can I use the information I am given?
Which strategy should I try?

- -

Solve

Did I follow the plan?
Did I show my work?
Did I write the answer?

- -

Check

Did I use the correct information?
Did I do what was asked?
Is my answer reasonable?

© Houghton Mifflin Harcourt Publishing Company and Stephen Hake

Facts   Simplify.

$6 + 6 \times 6 - 6 \div 6 =$	$3^2 + \sqrt{4} + 5(6) - 7 + 8 =$
$4 + 2(3 + 5) - 6 \div 2 =$	$2 + 2[3 + 4(7 - 5)] =$
$\sqrt{1^3 + 2^3 + 3^3} =$	$\dfrac{4 + 3(7 - 5)}{6 - (5 - 4)} =$
$(-3)(-3) + (-3) - (-3) =$	$\dfrac{3(-3) - (-3)(-3)}{(-3) - (3)(-3)} =$

Mental Math

a.	b.	c.	d.
e.	f.	g.	h.

Problem Solving

Understand
What information am I given?
What am I asked to find or do?

- -

Plan
How can I use the information I am given?
Which strategy should I try?

- -

Solve
Did I follow the plan?
Did I show my work?
Did I write the answer?

- -

Check
Did I use the correct information?
Did I do what was asked?
Is my answer reasonable?

© Houghton Mifflin Harcourt Publishing Company and Stephen Hake

Facts | Multiply.

9 ×8	8 ×2	10 ×10	6 ×3	4 ×2	5 ×5	9 ×9	6 ×4	9 ×6	7 ×3
9 ×3	6 ×5	0 ×0	7 ×6	8 ×8	7 ×4	5 ×3	9 ×7	2 ×2	8 ×6
7 ×7	6 ×2	4 ×3	8 ×5	4 ×4	3 ×2	n ×0	8 ×4	6 ×6	9 ×2
8 ×3	5 ×4	n ×1	7 ×2	9 ×5	8 ×7	3 ×3	9 ×4	5 ×2	7 ×5

Mental Math

a.	b.	c.	d.
e.	f.	g.	h.

Problem Solving

Understand
What information am I given?
What am I asked to find or do?

Plan
How can I use the information I am given?
Which strategy should I try?

Solve
Did I follow the plan?
Did I show my work?
Did I write the answer?

Check
Did I use the correct information?
Did I do what was asked?
Is my answer reasonable?

Saxon Math Course 2

© Houghton Mifflin Harcourt Publishing Company and Stephen Hake

Facts Simplify.

$6 + 6 \times 6 - 6 \div 6 =$	$3^2 + \sqrt{4} + 5(6) - 7 + 8 =$
$4 + 2(3 + 5) - 6 \div 2 =$	$2 + 2[3 + 4(7 - 5)] =$
$\sqrt{1^3 + 2^3 + 3^3} =$	$\dfrac{4 + 3(7 - 5)}{6 - (5 - 4)} =$
$(-3)(-3) + (-3) - (-3) =$	$\dfrac{3(-3) - (-3)(-3)}{(-3) - (3)(-3)} =$

Mental Math

a.	b.	c.	d.
e.	f.	g.	h.

Problem Solving

Understand
What information am I given?
What am I asked to find or do?

- -

Plan
How can I use the information I am given?
Which strategy should I try?

- -

Solve
Did I follow the plan?
Did I show my work?
Did I write the answer?

- -

Check
Did I use the correct information?
Did I do what was asked?
Is my answer reasonable?

© Houghton Mifflin Harcourt Publishing Company and Stephen Hake

Facts   Complete each step to solve each equation.

$2x + 5 = 45$	$3y + 4 = 22$	$5n - 3 = 12$	$3m - 7 = 14$
$2x =$	$3y =$	$5n =$	$3m =$
$x =$	$y =$	$n =$	$m =$
$15 = 3a - 6$	$24 = 2w + 6$	$-2x + 9 = 23$	$20 - 3y = 2$
$= 3a$	$= 2w$	$-2x =$	$-3y =$
$= a$	$= w$	$x =$	$y =$
$\frac{1}{2}m + 6 = 18$	$\frac{3}{4}n - 12 = 12$	$3y + 1.5 = 6$	$0.5w - 1.5 = 4.5$
$\frac{1}{2}m =$	$\frac{3}{4}n =$	$3y =$	$0.5w =$
$m =$	$n =$	$y =$	$w =$

Mental Math

a.	**b.**	**c.**	**d.**
e.	**f.**	**g.**	**h.**

Problem Solving

Understand

What information am I given?

What am I asked to find or do?

- -

Plan

How can I use the information I am given?

Which strategy should I try?

- -

Solve

Did I follow the plan?

Did I show my work?

Did I write the answer?

- -

Check

Did I use the correct information?

Did I do what was asked?

Is my answer reasonable?

© Houghton Mifflin Harcourt Publishing Company and Stephen Hake

Facts   Simplify.

$6 + 6 \times 6 - 6 \div 6 =$	$3^2 + \sqrt{4} + 5(6) - 7 + 8 =$
$4 + 2(3 + 5) - 6 \div 2 =$	$2 + 2[3 + 4(7 - 5)] =$
$\sqrt{1^3 + 2^3 + 3^3} =$	$\dfrac{4 + 3(7 - 5)}{6 - (5 - 4)} =$
$(-3)(-3) + (-3) - (-3) =$	$\dfrac{3(-3) - (-3)(-3)}{(-3) - (3)(-3)} =$

Mental Math

a.	**b.**	**c.**	**d.**
e.	**f.**	**g.**	**h.**

Problem Solving

Understand
What information am I given?
What am I asked to find or do?

Plan
How can I use the information I am given?
Which strategy should I try?

Solve
Did I follow the plan?
Did I show my work?
Did I write the answer?

Check
Did I use the correct information?
Did I do what was asked?
Is my answer reasonable?

© Houghton Mifflin Harcourt Publishing Company and Stephen Hake

Facts   Complete each step to solve each equation.

$2x + 5 = 45$	$3y + 4 = 22$	$5n - 3 = 12$	$3m - 7 = 14$
$2x =$	$3y =$	$5n =$	$3m =$
$x =$	$y =$	$n =$	$m =$
$15 = 3a - 6$	$24 = 2w + 6$	$-2x + 9 = 23$	$20 - 3y = 2$
$= 3a$	$= 2w$	$-2x =$	$-3y =$
$= a$	$= w$	$x =$	$y =$
$\frac{1}{2}m + 6 = 18$	$\frac{3}{4}n - 12 = 12$	$3y + 1.5 = 6$	$0.5w - 1.5 = 4.5$
$\frac{1}{2}m =$	$\frac{3}{4}n =$	$3y =$	$0.5w =$
$m =$	$n =$	$y =$	$w =$

Mental Math

a.	**b.**	**c.**	**d.**
e.	**f.**	**g.**	**h.**

Problem Solving

Understand

What information am I given?
What am I asked to find or do?

- -

Plan

How can I use the information I am given?
Which strategy should I try?

- -

Solve

Did I follow the plan?
Did I show my work?
Did I write the answer?

- -

Check

Did I use the correct information?
Did I do what was asked?
Is my answer reasonable?

© Houghton Mifflin Harcourt Publishing Company and Stephen Hake

Saxon Math Course 2

Facts Simplify.

$6 + 6 \times 6 - 6 \div 6 =$	$3^2 + \sqrt{4} + 5(6) - 7 + 8 =$
$4 + 2(3 + 5) - 6 \div 2 =$	$2 + 2[3 + 4(7 - 5)] =$
$\sqrt{1^3 + 2^3 + 3^3} =$	$\dfrac{4 + 3(7 - 5)}{6 - (5 - 4)} =$
$(-3)(-3) + (-3) - (-3) =$	$\dfrac{3(-3) - (-3)(-3)}{(-3) - (3)(-3)} =$

Mental Math

a.	b.	c.	d.
e.	f.	g.	h.

Problem Solving

Understand
What information am I given?
What am I asked to find or do?

Plan
How can I use the information I am given?
Which strategy should I try?

Solve
Did I follow the plan?
Did I show my work?
Did I write the answer?

Check
Did I use the correct information?
Did I do what was asked?
Is my answer reasonable?

© Houghton Mifflin Harcourt Publishing Company and Stephen Hake

Name _____ Time _____

Facts Complete each step to solve each equation.

$2x + 5 = 45$	$3y + 4 = 22$	$5n - 3 = 12$	$3m - 7 = 14$
$2x =$	$3y =$	$5n =$	$3m =$
$x =$	$y =$	$n =$	$m =$
$15 = 3a - 6$	$24 = 2w + 6$	$-2x + 9 = 23$	$20 - 3y = 2$
$= 3a$	$= 2w$	$-2x =$	$-3y =$
$= a$	$= w$	$x =$	$y =$
$\frac{1}{2}m + 6 = 18$	$\frac{3}{4}n - 12 = 12$	$3y + 1.5 = 6$	$0.5w - 1.5 = 4.5$
$\frac{1}{2}m =$	$\frac{3}{4}n =$	$3y =$	$0.5w =$
$m =$	$n =$	$y =$	$w =$

Mental Math

a.	b.	c.	d.
e.	f.	g.	h.

Problem Solving

Understand
What information am I given?
What am I asked to find or do?

- -

Plan
How can I use the information I am given?
Which strategy should I try?

- -

Solve
Did I follow the plan?
Did I show my work?
Did I write the answer?

- -

Check
Did I use the correct information?
Did I do what was asked?
Is my answer reasonable?

© Houghton Mifflin Harcourt Publishing Company and Stephen Hake

Saxon Math Course 2

Facts Write the equivalent decimal and fraction for each percent.

Percent	Decimal	Fraction	Percent	Decimal	Fraction
10%			$33\frac{1}{3}\%$		
90%			20%		
5%			75%		
$12\frac{1}{2}\%$			$66\frac{2}{3}\%$		
50%			1%		
25%			250%		

Mental Math

a.	b.	c.	d.
e.	f.	g.	h.

Problem Solving

Understand
What information am I given?
What am I asked to find or do?

Plan
How can I use the information I am given?
Which strategy should I try?

Solve
Did I follow the plan?
Did I show my work?
Did I write the answer?

Check
Did I use the correct information?
Did I do what was asked?
Is my answer reasonable?

© Houghton Mifflin Harcourt Publishing Company and Stephen Hake

Facts Complete each step to solve each equation.

$2x + 5 = 45$	$3y + 4 = 22$	$5n - 3 = 12$	$3m - 7 = 14$
$2x =$	$3y =$	$5n =$	$3m =$
$x =$	$y =$	$n =$	$m =$
$15 = 3a - 6$	$24 = 2w + 6$	$-2x + 9 = 23$	$20 - 3y = 2$
$= 3a$	$= 2w$	$-2x =$	$-3y =$
$= a$	$= w$	$x =$	$y =$
$\frac{1}{2}m + 6 = 18$	$\frac{3}{4}n - 12 = 12$	$3y + 1.5 = 6$	$0.5w - 1.5 = 4.5$
$\frac{1}{2}m =$	$\frac{3}{4}n =$	$3y =$	$0.5w =$
$m =$	$n =$	$y =$	$w =$

Mental Math

a.	**b.**	**c.**	**d.**
e.	**f.**	**g.**	**h.**

Problem Solving

Understand
What information am I given?
What am I asked to find or do?

Plan
How can I use the information I am given?
Which strategy should I try?

Solve
Did I follow the plan?
Did I show my work?
Did I write the answer?

Check
Did I use the correct information?
Did I do what was asked?
Is my answer reasonable?

© Houghton Mifflin Harcourt Publishing Company and Stephen Hake

Facts   Complete each step to solve each equation.

$2x + 5 = 45$	$3y + 4 = 22$	$5n - 3 = 12$	$3m - 7 = 14$
$2x =$	$3y =$	$5n =$	$3m =$
$x =$	$y =$	$n =$	$m =$
$15 = 3a - 6$	$24 = 2w + 6$	$-2x + 9 = 23$	$20 - 3y = 2$
$= 3a$	$= 2w$	$-2x =$	$-3y =$
$= a$	$= w$	$x =$	$y =$
$\frac{1}{2}m + 6 = 18$	$\frac{3}{4}n - 12 = 12$	$3y + 1.5 = 6$	$0.5w - 1.5 = 4.5$
$\frac{1}{2}m =$	$\frac{3}{4}n =$	$3y =$	$0.5w =$
$m =$	$n =$	$y =$	$w =$

Mental Math

a.	**b.**	**c.**	**d.**
e.	**f.**	**g.**	**h.**

Problem Solving

Understand
What information am I given?
What am I asked to find or do?

- -

Plan
How can I use the information I am given?
Which strategy should I try?

- -

Solve
Did I follow the plan?
Did I show my work?
Did I write the answer?

- -

Check
Did I use the correct information?
Did I do what was asked?
Is my answer reasonable?

© Houghton Mifflin Harcourt Publishing Company and Stephen Hake

Facts   Solve each equation.

$6x + 2x =$	$6x - 2x =$	$(6x)(2x) =$	$\dfrac{6x}{2x} =$
$9xy + 3xy =$	$9xy - 3xy =$	$(9xy)(3xy) =$	$\dfrac{9xy}{3xy} =$
$x + y + x =$	$x + y - x =$	$(x)(y)(-x) =$	$\dfrac{xy}{x} =$
$3x + x + 3 =$	$3x - x - 3 =$	$(3x)(-x)(-3) =$	$\dfrac{(2x)(8xy)}{4y} =$

Mental Math

a.	**b.**	**c.**	**d.**
e.	**f.**	**g.**	**h.**

Problem Solving

Understand
What information am I given?
What am I asked to find or do?

Plan
How can I use the information I am given?
Which strategy should I try?

Solve
Did I follow the plan?
Did I show my work?
Did I write the answer?

Check
Did I use the correct information?
Did I do what was asked?
Is my answer reasonable?

© Houghton Mifflin Harcourt Publishing Company and Stephen Hake

Facts Write the equivalent decimal and fraction for each percent.

Percent	Decimal	Fraction	Percent	Decimal	Fraction
10%			$33\frac{1}{3}\%$		
90%			20%		
5%			75%		
$12\frac{1}{2}\%$			$66\frac{2}{3}\%$		
50%			1%		
25%			250%		

Mental Math

a.	b.	c.	d.
e.	f.	g.	h.

Problem Solving

Understand

What information am I given?

What am I asked to find or do?

Plan

How can I use the information I am given?

Which strategy should I try?

Solve

Did I follow the plan?

Did I show my work?

Did I write the answer?

Check

Did I use the correct information?

Did I do what was asked?

Is my answer reasonable?

© Houghton Mifflin Harcourt Publishing Company and Stephen Hake

Facts	Solve each equation.		
$6x + 2x =$	$6x - 2x =$	$(6x)(2x) =$	$\dfrac{6x}{2x} =$
$9xy + 3xy =$	$9xy - 3xy =$	$(9xy)(3xy) =$	$\dfrac{9xy}{3xy} =$
$x + y + x =$	$x + y - x =$	$(x)(y)(-x) =$	$\dfrac{xy}{x} =$
$3x + x + 3 =$	$3x - x - 3 =$	$(3x)(-x)(-3) =$	$\dfrac{(2x)(8xy)}{4y} =$

Mental Math			
a.	**b.**	**c.**	**d.**
e.	**f.**	**g.**	**h.**

Problem Solving

Understand
What information am I given?
What am I asked to find or do?

Plan
How can I use the information I am given?
Which strategy should I try?

Solve
Did I follow the plan?
Did I show my work?
Did I write the answer?

Check
Did I use the correct information?
Did I do what was asked?
Is my answer reasonable?

© Houghton Mifflin Harcourt Publishing Company and Stephen Hake

Facts   Write the equivalent decimal and fraction for each percent.

Percent	Decimal	Fraction	Percent	Decimal	Fraction
10%			$33\frac{1}{3}\%$		
90%			20%		
5%			75%		
$12\frac{1}{2}\%$			$66\frac{2}{3}\%$		
50%			1%		
25%			250%		

Mental Math

a.	b.	c.	d.
e.	f.	g.	h.

Problem Solving

Understand
What information am I given?
What am I asked to find or do?

Plan
How can I use the information I am given?
Which strategy should I try?

Solve
Did I follow the plan?
Did I show my work?
Did I write the answer?

Check
Did I use the correct information?
Did I do what was asked?
Is my answer reasonable?

© Houghton Mifflin Harcourt Publishing Company and Stephen Hake

Facts   Solve each equation.

$6x + 2x =$	$6x - 2x =$	$(6x)(2x) =$	$\dfrac{6x}{2x} =$
$9xy + 3xy =$	$9xy - 3xy =$	$(9xy)(3xy) =$	$\dfrac{9xy}{3xy} =$
$x + y + x =$	$x + y - x =$	$(x)(y)(-x) =$	$\dfrac{xy}{x} =$
$3x + x + 3 =$	$3x - x - 3 =$	$(3x)(-x)(-3) =$	$\dfrac{(2x)(8xy)}{4y} =$

Mental Math

a.	**b.**	**c.**	**d.**
e.	**f.**	**g.**	**h.**

Problem Solving

Understand
What information am I given?
What am I asked to find or do?

Plan
How can I use the information I am given?
Which strategy should I try?

Solve
Did I follow the plan?
Did I show my work?
Did I write the answer?

Check
Did I use the correct information?
Did I do what was asked?
Is my answer reasonable?

© Houghton Mifflin Harcourt Publishing Company and Stephen Hake

Facts   Solve each equation.

$6x + 2x =$	$6x - 2x =$	$(6x)(2x) =$	$\dfrac{6x}{2x} =$
$9xy + 3xy =$	$9xy - 3xy =$	$(9xy)(3xy) =$	$\dfrac{9xy}{3xy} =$
$x + y + x =$	$x + y - x =$	$(x)(y)(-x) =$	$\dfrac{xy}{x} =$
$3x + x + 3 =$	$3x - x - 3 =$	$(3x)(-x)(-3) =$	$\dfrac{(2x)(8xy)}{4y} =$

Mental Math

a.	b.	c.	d.
e.	f.	g.	h.

Problem Solving

Understand
What information am I given?
What am I asked to find or do?

Plan
How can I use the information I am given?
Which strategy should I try?

Solve
Did I follow the plan?
Did I show my work?
Did I write the answer?

Check
Did I use the correct information?
Did I do what was asked?
Is my answer reasonable?

© Houghton Mifflin Harcourt Publishing Company and Stephen Hake

Name _____ Time _____

Facts Write the equivalent decimal and fraction for each percent.

Percent	Decimal	Fraction	Percent	Decimal	Fraction
10%			$33\frac{1}{3}\%$		
90%			20%		
5%			75%		
$12\frac{1}{2}\%$			$66\frac{2}{3}\%$		
50%			1%		
25%			250%		

Mental Math

a.	b.	c.	d.
e.	f.	g.	h.

Problem Solving

Understand
What information am I given?
What am I asked to find or do?

Plan
How can I use the information I am given?
Which strategy should I try?

Solve
Did I follow the plan?
Did I show my work?
Did I write the answer?

Check
Did I use the correct information?
Did I do what was asked?
Is my answer reasonable?

© Houghton Mifflin Harcourt Publishing Company and Stephen Hake

Saxon Math Course 2

Name _____ Time _____

Facts   Solve each equation.

$6x + 2x =$	$6x - 2x =$	$(6x)(2x) =$	$\dfrac{6x}{2x} =$
$9xy + 3xy =$	$9xy - 3xy =$	$(9xy)(3xy) =$	$\dfrac{9xy}{3xy} =$
$x + y + x =$	$x + y - x =$	$(x)(y)(-x) =$	$\dfrac{xy}{x} =$
$3x + x + 3 =$	$3x - x - 3 =$	$(3x)(-x)(-3) =$	$\dfrac{(2x)(8xy)}{4y} =$

Mental Math

a.	**b.**	**c.**	**d.**
e.	**f.**	**g.**	**h.**

Problem Solving

Understand
What information am I given?
What am I asked to find or do?

Plan
How can I use the information I am given?
Which strategy should I try?

Solve
Did I follow the plan?
Did I show my work?
Did I write the answer?

Check
Did I use the correct information?
Did I do what was asked?
Is my answer reasonable?

© Houghton Mifflin Harcourt Publishing Company and Stephen Hake

Name _____ Time _____

Facts   Simplify. Write each answer in scientific notation.

$(1 \times 10^6)(1 \times 10^6) =$	$(3 \times 10^3)(3 \times 10^3) =$	$(4 \times 10^{-5})(2 \times 10^{-6}) =$
$(5 \times 10^5)(5 \times 10^5) =$	$(6 \times 10^{-3})(7 \times 10^{-4}) =$	$(3 \times 10^6)(2 \times 10^{-4}) =$
$\dfrac{8 \times 10^8}{2 \times 10^2} =$	$\dfrac{5 \times 10^6}{2 \times 10^3} =$	$\dfrac{9 \times 10^3}{3 \times 10^8} =$
$\dfrac{2 \times 10^6}{4 \times 10^2} =$	$\dfrac{1 \times 10^{-3}}{4 \times 10^8} =$	$\dfrac{8 \times 10^{-8}}{2 \times 10^{-2}} =$

Mental Math

a.	b.	c.	d.
e.	f.	g.	h.

Problem Solving

Understand
What information am I given?
What am I asked to find or do?

Plan
How can I use the information I am given?
Which strategy should I try?

Solve
Did I follow the plan?
Did I show my work?
Did I write the answer?

Check
Did I use the correct information?
Did I do what was asked?
Is my answer reasonable?

© Houghton Mifflin Harcourt Publishing Company and Stephen Hake

Facts Solve each equation.

$6x + 2x =$	$6x - 2x =$	$(6x)(2x) =$	$\dfrac{6x}{2x} =$
$9xy + 3xy =$	$9xy - 3xy =$	$(9xy)(3xy) =$	$\dfrac{9xy}{3xy} =$
$x + y + x =$	$x + y - x =$	$(x)(y)(-x) =$	$\dfrac{xy}{x} =$
$3x + x + 3 =$	$3x - x - 3 =$	$(3x)(-x)(-3) =$	$\dfrac{(2x)(8xy)}{4y} =$

Mental Math

a.	**b.**	**c.**	**d.**
e.	**f.**	**g.**	**h.**

Problem Solving

Understand

What information am I given?

What am I asked to find or do?

- -

Plan

How can I use the information I am given?

Which strategy should I try?

- -

Solve

Did I follow the plan?

Did I show my work?

Did I write the answer?

- -

Check

Did I use the correct information?

Did I do what was asked?

Is my answer reasonable?

© Houghton Mifflin Harcourt Publishing Company and Stephen Hake

Facts Solve each equation.

$6x + 2x =$	$6x - 2x =$	$(6x)(2x) =$	$\dfrac{6x}{2x} =$
$9xy + 3xy =$	$9xy - 3xy =$	$(9xy)(3xy) =$	$\dfrac{9xy}{3xy} =$
$x + y + x =$	$x + y - x =$	$(x)(y)(-x) =$	$\dfrac{xy}{x} =$
$3x + x + 3 =$	$3x - x - 3 =$	$(3x)(-x)(-3) =$	$\dfrac{(2x)(8xy)}{4y} =$

Mental Math

a.	b.	c.	d.
e.	f.	g.	h.

Problem Solving

Understand
What information am I given?
What am I asked to find or do?

- -

Plan
How can I use the information I am given?
Which strategy should I try?

- -

Solve
Did I follow the plan?
Did I show my work?
Did I write the answer?

- -

Check
Did I use the correct information?
Did I do what was asked?
Is my answer reasonable?

© Houghton Mifflin Harcourt Publishing Company and Stephen Hake

Facts Solve each equation.

$6x + 2x =$	$6x - 2x =$	$(6x)(2x) =$	$\dfrac{6x}{2x} =$
$9xy + 3xy =$	$9xy - 3xy =$	$(9xy)(3xy) =$	$\dfrac{9xy}{3xy}$
$x + y + x =$	$x + y - x =$	$(x)(y)(-x) =$	$\dfrac{xy}{x} =$
$3x + x + 3 =$	$3x - x - 3 =$	$(3x)(-x)(-3) =$	$\dfrac{(2x)(8xy)}{4y} =$

Mental Math

a.	**b.**	**c.**	**d.**
e.	**f.**	**g.**	**h.**

Problem Solving

Understand

What information am I given?

What am I asked to find or do?

Plan

How can I use the information I am given?

Which strategy should I try?

Solve

Did I follow the plan?

Did I show my work?

Did I write the answer?

Check

Did I use the correct information?

Did I do what was asked?

Is my answer reasonable?

© Houghton Mifflin Harcourt Publishing Company and Stephen Hake

© Houghton Mifflin Harcourt Publishing Company and Stephen Hake

Facts   Simplify. Write each answer in scientific notation.

$(1 \times 10^6)(1 \times 10^6) =$	$(3 \times 10^3)(3 \times 10^3) =$	$(4 \times 10^{-5})(2 \times 10^{-6}) =$
$(5 \times 10^5)(5 \times 10^5) =$	$(6 \times 10^{-3})(7 \times 10^{-4}) =$	$(3 \times 10^6)(2 \times 10^{-4}) =$
$\dfrac{8 \times 10^8}{2 \times 10^2} =$	$\dfrac{5 \times 10^6}{2 \times 10^3} =$	$\dfrac{9 \times 10^3}{3 \times 10^8} =$
$\dfrac{2 \times 10^6}{4 \times 10^2} =$	$\dfrac{1 \times 10^{-3}}{4 \times 10^8} =$	$\dfrac{8 \times 10^{-8}}{2 \times 10^{-2}} =$

Mental Math

a.	**b.**	**c.**	**d.**
e.	**f.**	**g.**	**h.**

Problem Solving

Understand
What information am I given?
What am I asked to find or do?

Plan
How can I use the information I am given?
Which strategy should I try?

Solve
Did I follow the plan?
Did I show my work?
Did I write the answer?

Check
Did I use the correct information?
Did I do what was asked?
Is my answer reasonable?

Facts   Solve each equation.

$6x + 2x =$	$6x - 2x =$	$(6x)(2x) =$	$\dfrac{6x}{2x} =$
$9xy + 3xy =$	$9xy - 3xy =$	$(9xy)(3xy) =$	$\dfrac{9xy}{3xy} =$
$x + y + x =$	$x + y - x =$	$(x)(y)(-x) =$	$\dfrac{xy}{x} =$
$3x + x + 3 =$	$3x - x - 3 =$	$(3x)(-x)(-3) =$	$\dfrac{(2x)(8xy)}{4y} =$

Mental Math

a.	b.	c.	d.
e.	**f.**	**g.**	**h.**

Problem Solving

Understand

What information am I given?
What am I asked to find or do?

- -

Plan

How can I use the information I am given?
Which strategy should I try?

- -

Solve

Did I follow the plan?
Did I show my work?
Did I write the answer?

- -

Check

Did I use the correct information?
Did I do what was asked?
Is my answer reasonable?

© Houghton Mifflin Harcourt Publishing Company and Stephen Hake

Facts	Simplify. Write each answer in scientific notation.

$(1 \times 10^6)(1 \times 10^6) =$	$(3 \times 10^3)(3 \times 10^3) =$	$(4 \times 10^{-5})(2 \times 10^{-6}) =$
$(5 \times 10^5)(5 \times 10^5) =$	$(6 \times 10^{-3})(7 \times 10^{-4}) =$	$(3 \times 10^6)(2 \times 10^{-4}) =$
$\dfrac{8 \times 10^8}{2 \times 10^2} =$	$\dfrac{5 \times 10^6}{2 \times 10^3} =$	$\dfrac{9 \times 10^3}{3 \times 10^8} =$
$\dfrac{2 \times 10^6}{4 \times 10^2} =$	$\dfrac{1 \times 10^{-3}}{4 \times 10^8} =$	$\dfrac{8 \times 10^{-8}}{2 \times 10^{-2}} =$

Mental Math

a.	b.	c.	d.
e.	f.	g.	h.

Problem Solving

Understand
What information am I given?
What am I asked to find or do?

Plan
How can I use the information I am given?
Which strategy should I try?

Solve
Did I follow the plan?
Did I show my work?
Did I write the answer?

Check
Did I use the correct information?
Did I do what was asked?
Is my answer reasonable?

© Houghton Mifflin Harcourt Publishing Company and Stephen Hake

Facts   Solve each equation.

$6x + 2x =$	$6x - 2x =$	$(6x)(2x) =$	$\dfrac{6x}{2x} =$
$9xy + 3xy =$	$9xy - 3xy =$	$(9xy)(3xy) =$	$\dfrac{9xy}{3xy} =$
$x + y + x =$	$x + y - x =$	$(x)(y)(-x) =$	$\dfrac{xy}{x} =$
$3x + x + 3 =$	$3x - x - 3 =$	$(3x)(-x)(-3) =$	$\dfrac{(2x)(8xy)}{4y} =$

Mental Math

a.	b.	c.	d.
e.	f.	g.	h.

Problem Solving

Understand
What information am I given?
What am I asked to find or do?

- -

Plan
How can I use the information I am given?
Which strategy should I try?

- -

Solve
Did I follow the plan?
Did I show my work?
Did I write the answer?

- -

Check
Did I use the correct information?
Did I do what was asked?
Is my answer reasonable?

© Houghton Mifflin Harcourt Publishing Company and Stephen Hake

Name _____ Time _____

Facts Simplify. Write each answer in scientific notation.

$(1 \times 10^6)(1 \times 10^6) =$	$(3 \times 10^3)(3 \times 10^3) =$	$(4 \times 10^{-5})(2 \times 10^{-6}) =$
$(5 \times 10^5)(5 \times 10^5) =$	$(6 \times 10^{-3})(7 \times 10^{-4}) =$	$(3 \times 10^6)(2 \times 10^{-4}) =$
$\dfrac{8 \times 10^8}{2 \times 10^2} =$	$\dfrac{5 \times 10^6}{2 \times 10^3} =$	$\dfrac{9 \times 10^3}{3 \times 10^8} =$
$\dfrac{2 \times 10^6}{4 \times 10^2} =$	$\dfrac{1 \times 10^{-3}}{4 \times 10^8} =$	$\dfrac{8 \times 10^{-8}}{2 \times 10^{-2}} =$

Mental Math

a.	**b.**	**c.**	**d.**
e.	**f.**	**g.**	**h.**

Problem Solving

Understand
What information am I given?
What am I asked to find or do?

Plan
How can I use the information I am given?
Which strategy should I try?

Solve
Did I follow the plan?
Did I show my work?
Did I write the answer?

Check
Did I use the correct information?
Did I do what was asked?
Is my answer reasonable?

© Houghton Mifflin Harcourt Publishing Company and Stephen Hake